"*Building Bridges* fills a profound gap in biblical counseling literature and is by far one of the most informed, thoughtful, and practical guides I have ever read on counseling children and teens. Lowe's creativity in transitioning the riches of biblical counseling and theology into a practical form that helps counselors effectively draw out the hearts of some of our most cherished is unmatched. As a practitioner of almost twenty years, this book serves as a much needed and appreciated gift!"

Jeremy Lelek, President, Association of Biblical Counselors

"Now and again, an exceptional book comes out that will prove to be a classic on a topic. Julie Lowe's *Building Bridges* is bound to become a classic biblical counseling resource for helping children and teens. Julie packs gospel-centered, grace-saturated truth in every chapter and ends the book with a trove of helpful exercises and worksheets. Pastors, youth and children's workers, and parents should get a copy, read it, and deploy the wisdom from its pages."

Marty Machowski, Pastor; author of *The Ology, Parenting First Aid, God Made Boys and Girls*, and other gospel-centered resources for church and home

"For those of us who sometimes feel a bit lost in knowing how to winsomely connect with and get to know the hearts of the children we counsel, Julie Lowe has given us a very helpful resource. *Building Bridges* is full of extremely useful ideas and activities for gaining entry and speaking God's truth into the lives of hurting children. Anyone who wants to grow in their skills in counseling children will want a copy of this book."

Amy Baker, Editor of *Caring for the Souls of Children*, Faith Resources

"Julie Lowe's *Building Bridges* brings biblical ministry to children to a new level of understanding and practice! This tool will become standard fare in BJU Seminary's course on counseling children and adolescents. Packed with case wisdom, biblical insight, and creative activities, this is the finest text available for discovering and ministering to the hearts of children in the counseling room. I highly recommend it."

Jim Berg, Professor of biblical counseling at BJU Seminary; executive director of Freedom That Lasts®, a local church-based addiction recovery program; author of *Changed Into His Image, God is More Than Enough, Essential Virtues*, and *Help! I'm Addicted*

"Today there is a cacophony of voices, whether books, articles, or blogs bellowing, '*This* is how you parent. *This* is the secret formula to make your kids turn out right.' Into this riot steps Julie Lowe. Eschewing false promises, *Building Bridges* offers wisdom—a broad framework for understanding children and their struggles as well as practical strategies for connecting with them. A triumph!"

Benjamin Crawford, Psychiatrist at Riverside Counseling Center

"This book is as theologically rich as it is practical. Julie takes great effort to be biblically sound in her approach to counseling and also takes just as much effort to give detailed examples of practical exercises to engage children. For any parent or youth worker that's struggling to reach a specific child or student, this book will be a great resource."

John Perritt, Director of Resources for Reformed Youth Ministries; author of *Mark: How Jesus Changes Everything* and *Insecure: Fighting Our Lesser Fears with a Greater One*; editor of the Track series

"Genuine love begins with taking the time to truly know someone. This is especially true as we seek to love those God calls us to counsel and minister to. In *Building Bridges*, Julie Lowe provides a treasure trove of practical activities and illustrations that are specifically designed to help us know and speak the truth of the gospel to the children and youth God has placed in our lives. I am eminently more prepared to love the children in my church (and in my home) as a result of having this resource."

Scott Mehl, Pastor, Cornerstone Church of West L.A.; author of *Loving Messy People*

"It is impossible with a few words to capture the love, wisdom, and practical helpfulness that splashes across every page of *Building Bridges*. If you are a parent and you want to know how to love and be God's tool of change in the lives of your children, you should read this book. If you are a teacher, children's counselor, or in children's or youth ministry, this book is absolutely essential for you. As a father of adult children, I read *Building Bridges* with gratitude for the many that it will help, but also with sadness that I didn't have it when our children were young. We cannot lose another generation of vulnerable children, made in the image of God, to the evils of life in this broken, groaning world, and for this reason, I enthusiastically commend *Building Bridges* to you."

Paul David Tripp, Pastor; author; international conference speaker

"'Tell me about your problems,' rarely gives us access to children because words can elude them when emotions are complicated. Julie has given us creative and engaging means of drawing out a child's heart."

Edward T. Welch, Faculty and counselor, Christian Counseling and Educational Foundation (CCEF); author of *A Small Book about a Big Problem*

"Counseling children and teens provides unique challenges to even the most gifted biblical counselors. Children and teens think and operate differently than adults, and connecting with them and understanding what lies within their hearts requires distinctive skills. *Building Bridges* is here to help. Julie Lowe has provided an excellent resource to explain the why, what, and how of connecting the truths of Scripture with the hearts of children and teens. Counselors, teachers, parents, Sunday school workers, and youth ministry workers will all benefit from the wealth of knowledge and tools in this work."

C.W. Solomon, Executive Director, Biblical Counseling Coalition

"What a treasure Julie has given to the church and to parents in her latest book, *Building Bridges*. With the conviction that every child is an image-bearer of the living God, Julie offers practical exercises, tools, and methods to draw out your child in conversation. In a culture that is quickly forgetting the art of conversation, Julie draws our gaze back to Scripture and shows us Jesus's heart for children. I am confident this book will bless and impact many families for the kingdom of God."

  Jonathan D. Holmes, Executive Director, Fieldstone Counseling; pastor of counseling, Parkside Church

"Truth be told, children and adolescents who are struggling with life often leave parents, teachers, youth ministry staff, and counselors mystified. Julie Lowe understands this and has written a book that is intended to fill in the gap between the theologically profound and the how-to practical. *Building Bridges* grounds the process of counseling children in a model that is not based on behavioral modification language but on the language of the gospel. Parenting, after all, is the most challenging form of discipleship that there is. *Building Bridges* provides the reader with a pattern of entering and exploring the life of a child and in that context winning their trust, providing hope to their heart, and offering a pathway to change."

  Jeffrey S. Black, Professor and Chair, Department of Counseling & Psychology, Cairn University; licensed psychologist; director of counseling services, Oasis Center

Building Bridges

BIBLICAL COUNSELING ACTIVITIES
FOR CHILDREN AND TEENS

Julie Lowe

New
Growth
Press

newgrowthpress.com

New Growth Press, Greensboro, NC 27404
newgrowthpress.com
Copyright © 2020 by Julie Lowe

Cover Design: Faceout Books, faceoutstudio.com
Interior Typesetting and eBook: LParnell Book Services

ISBN: 978-1-64507-050-4 (Print)
ISBN: 978-1-64507-052-8 (eBook)

Library of Congress Cataloging-in-Publication Data on File

Printed in China

27 26 25 24 23 22 21 20   1 2 3 4 5

Contents

Chapter 1

Working with Children and Teens Requires a Different Approach

Tiana was a lonely teenager who had participated in "sexting" online, in order to fit in with a group from school. Unfortunately, that same group of "friends" circulated her pictures around school, eventually landing her in front of a detective, her parents, and the school administration.

Tiana was initially angry, resistant, and untrusting toward counseling. She did not believe anyone really cared. After several sessions of getting to know her, listening well, and finding ways into her world, Tiana shared that she connected best through music. I asked if she would be willing to share some songs and lyrics that reflected how she felt. We jumped on my computer and listened together.

After one song finished playing on the computer screen, Tiana sat back, nodding her head, as if in agreement. I asked, "How does this song connect to your life?"

Tiana quickly responded, "Well, I guess I feel like everyone has someone but me, just like the song says. So what do I have?"

"I'm sure it does feel that way, Tiana. It's hard when it feels like everyone around you has a boyfriend or a group where they feel they belong. The question is, is our meaning and worth found in a boyfriend or peer group? Can we only feel valued if another human finds us valuable?"

Tiana thought for a moment. "I know the right answer should be that God is all I need . . . but I want to be accepted by my friends, too. I don't want to be alone."

I nodded and replied, "I don't want to be alone either, and you and I are never really alone. I know it is hard to believe, but the Lord is right there and he cares. He sees your sadness, he knows how you feel and he sympathizes with you."

I paused and watched Tiana tear up. "I can't promise that people will treat you the way they should—or the way you want them to treat you—but I can promise that the Lord will never leave you, never forsake you, and that he will take every hard and lonely moment in your life and use it for good." Tears streamed down Tiana's face. My words were equally comforting and hard to hear. "I know it does not get rid of the pain of rejection, but it does help lessen it when we learn to embrace and long for God's love, more than the approval of other people.

"What do you think about the both of us finding a song that speaks to God's never-ending love when others fail us? We can both do some research and next week compare what we've found." Tiana agreed, and I encouraged her to share her assignment with her parents; perhaps they'd have some helpful ideas as well. It was the first time Tiana had made herself vulnerable, and the first sign she was willing to engage honestly. What was once a godless vision of her future began revealing a glimpse of hope.

Several sessions later, Tiana not only found songs that shifted to a more Christ-centered perspective; she began writing her own music in counseling—music that moved from despair toward trusting the Lord and finding comfort in his love. Her circumstances had not yet changed, but her outlook was being transformed. Tiana was learning to find worth in the One who made her. She was slowly becoming more vulnerable with her parents and choosing to let go of the friends she once would do anything to impress.

* * *

Young people like Tiana need wise adults who are willing to enter their world and experiences. They need us to sit with them and feel what life is like in their shoes, and they need a vision for something beyond such experiences. They need hope that there is more to their lives than their current circumstances, and they need us to find winsome ways to point them to the Lord.

As caring adults, it is both a privilege and responsibility to consider how we can woo a younger generation to the Lord. It must always be our goal to aptly apply Scripture to the uniqueness of each child, teen, or family. Biblical principles are unchanging; they are always at work and always effective; and we must continually be working to thoughtfully apply them to the needs of the moment. We want our wise, loving, godly care to be both vibrant and improvising, engaging and appealing. We need to take the time to help young people know what godly responses look like in the particulars of their experiences. The next generation needs to know that God really has given them everything they need for life (2 Peter 1:3).

This book aspires to help counselors, families, and other caring adults to build bridges—life-giving, gospel-infused connections—with young people in our sphere of influence. With each new generation, we have a biblical charge to teach young people the ways of the Lord. We are charged with bringing Scripture to life for each child and teen (Deuteronomy 6:4–6). In a culture where children and teens are increasingly looking to their own peers as the source of truth and knowledge, meaningful relationships with positive, wise adults will steer young people toward biblical answers to their questions and struggles.

Ministering to children and teens is different from ministering to adults. Many counselors avoid counseling children, knowing it requires a different approach. It is true that we can often make the mistake of relating to children as we do with adults. Many young people simply cannot interact at an adult level. If we want kids and teens to open up about their world, and if we want to minister to them effectively, we need to connect to them in a way that makes them feel understood and known. This means we do what we can to meet them where they are developmentally. It requires working hard to see life through their eyes. This practice reflects the heart of Jesus, who reminded us that we must become like children to enter the kingdom of heaven and that whoever receives a child in his name receives him (Matthew 18:2–4).

It is valuable to know young people both individually and developmentally. We can then speak into their world and help them understand themselves and their need for the Lord. At the same time, it's important to remember that the temptations, struggles and needs of the human heart remain the same regardless of the stage of life. The soul needs to be nurtured with gospel truth at any age. Each individual needs to know Jesus and learn about God's love and care at every age. Everyone needs to be challenged to love God and people. But even though biblical wisdom and principles are unchanging, the way we contextualize them and apply them to children is not always the same.

As adults, we often find it difficult to connect personally to young people. It can feel hard to draw them out or engage them in meaningful conversations. The disconnect usually revolves around our expectations—trying to have an adult conversation with a child, assuming teens are interested in what we are interested in, talking down to them, expecting them to be able to talk up to us, or making young people sit and have a conversation about things that have no felt interest or significance to them.

As counselors, some of us may feel more successful at connecting with children and teenagers than we actually are. We naively walk away from interactions feeling semi-successful. We kept the conversation going, got him or her to answer our questions, and may have even addressed a few struggles in his or her life. We may walk away from a session like this and think it went fairly well. However, when you ask the young person how it was, you might get a very different story: "It was awful. Boring. I hate counseling and don't want to go back." The young person might walk away from such a session feeling as though someone just pulled their teeth, and they will do what they can to avoid another painful visit.

We want our bonds with others to come easily, effortlessly, and naturally. We want people to like us. We may even presume our counselees can or should be on the same intellectual, emotional, spiritual, or social level we are. But an effortless connection or shared understanding is rarely the case with any counselee, much less a child. We mistakenly believe that good relationships always come effortlessly and that hard work shouldn't be needed. When we think this way, we forget the lengths to which Jesus extended himself to love, share, and connect with us. He came down to us, and he continues to meet us in our weakness, feebleness, and childishness. He took on human flesh, humbling himself and entering into our experience, even experiencing death in our place (Philippians 2:6–8).

In light of everything Jesus has done for us, Scripture likewise urges us, "Do nothing out of selfish ambition or vain conceit. Rather, in humility value others above yourselves, not looking to your own interests but each of you to the interests of others" (Philippians 2:3–4, NIV). In our relationships with one another, we are called to have the mindset of Christ Jesus. How can we model this heart of Jesus in our interactions with the young people we counsel? What would it look like to approach kids and teens with the mindset of Christ Jesus?

We start by being committed to meeting young people where they are, not where *we* are, nor where we want them to be. We must be willing to work hard and thoughtfully to enter into their world. This will mean taking time to sit, observe, listen, and help children and teenagers feel known. It is not until we do this that we will have won the trust needed to influence them for the gospel.

I often tell the counseling students I train that their ability to work well with adults does not mean they will be competent to work well with children or teenagers. However, if they can learn to work with young people, they will likely be better equipped and skillful at working with adults. Why? Because they will have spent extra time learning the unnatural skill of entering into another person's world, striving to both know and love him or her well.

DRAWING OUT CHILDREN AND TEENS

Drawing out young people means striving to unearth what is going on in their hearts and minds. We are uncovering their motives, desires, fears, hopes, temptations, and dreams. As Proverbs 20:5 says, "The purpose in a man's heart is like deep water, but a man of understanding will draw it out." That is our goal: to draw out the purposes of the heart, and then speak truth back in.

When drawing out a child or teen, often it is the skill of an adult that determines how effective counseling is, more so than the ability of a young person to articulate his or her inner world. We tend to chat with a child and be tempted to conclude after a few minutes that they lack insight, thoughtful responses, or even care about their situation. We tell ourselves that we tried to gain insight but that the child just lacks personal awareness or is unwilling to open up. Unfortunately, much of the time we are wrong. Given genuine care, consistent pursuit, winsome approaches, the patience of a listening ear, and the willingness to ask good questions, young people can and do share deeply.

It's not until you start to know a young person well that you can contextualize truth to meet their particular needs. This is a step that can never be skipped. Jesus modeled the idea of knowing people individually. In his life on earth, Jesus modeled specific care and personal interaction to those he encountered. The woman at the well was known intimately and given grace despite her many sins (John 4). Zacchaeus, a tax collector, was sought out for fellowship (Luke 19). The Pharisees and Sadducees were rebuked and called a brood of vipers (Matthew 12). The little children were told to come and were embraced (Luke 18). Each disciple was known individually (John 1:42, 47). Jesus often demonstrated that he knew his followers so well that he knew what they were thinking (Mark 9:33–34). He spoke to their doubts, fear, unbelief, *and* devotion (Matthew 8:26).

Be an expert at knowing the child in front of you

We have a Father who knows us personally, intimately and completely. He created us, he formed us, and he knows the depths of our hearts. He can go places inside our heads and hearts no one else can reach, and he meets us there. We are called to model the love of God by seeking to know the children and teenagers we are interacting with in the same ways that God knows us.

Consider Psalm 139, beginning with verses 1–5:

> O LORD, you have searched me and known me!
> You know when I sit down and when I rise up;
>   you discern my thoughts from afar.
> You search out my path and my lying down
>   and are acquainted with all my ways.
> Even before a word is on my tongue,
>   behold, O LORD, you know it altogether.
> You hem me in, behind and before,
>   and lay your hand upon me.

Verses 13–18 go on to describe how well he knows you and I:

> For you formed my inward parts;
>   you knitted me together in my mother's womb.
> I praise you, for I am fearfully and wonderfully made.
> Wonderful are your works;
>   my soul knows it very well.
> My frame was not hidden from you,

> when I was being made in secret,
>> intricately woven in the depths of the earth.
> Your eyes saw my unformed substance;
> in your book were written, every one of them,
>> the days that were formed for me,
>> when as yet there was none of them.
> How precious to me are your thoughts, O God!
>> How vast is the sum of them!
> If I would count them, they are more than the sand.
>> I awake, and I am still with you.

In counseling or personal ministry, we learn to understand the nature of certain struggles, experiences, and emotional reactions. We pay attention to themes and motives, interpersonal and intrapersonal dynamics, and we learn how to speak into such things with biblical skill and wisdom. However, it is equally important that we treat each young person we work with as a distinct person. This means we make the effort to see him or her as a unique individual whom we strive to understand. It means that in imitation of our heavenly Father who knows us intimately, we commit to knowing the particular child or teenager in front of us. It means we take our time not just to know the struggle, but the person behind the struggle.

Each young person has innate traits that form, motivate, and influence his or her behaviors and intentions. Who are they? What makes them tick? What motivates them or discourages them? How can we speak to them, encourage, confront, or comfort in a way that is beneficial to this person? It requires us to build trust and bridges so that we both genuinely know and understand the individual before us.

The pursuit of knowing young people well compels us to become people of wisdom and understanding. We strive to know their strengths, weaknesses, limitations, and temptations. We consider each family, lifestyle, parenting style, and the impact of these factors in children's lives. Equipped with this understanding, we then look for godly ways to speak wisely and lovingly into these areas of their lives and to nurture their growth in godliness. Thoughtful, effective counseling mirrors insight back to each child and teen so that they may know themselves better and see their need for Christ.

A framework for understanding the heart

To develop a wise and biblical understanding of children, we need to have a foundational understanding of human nature. My colleague Mike Emlet has written extensively about the biblical view of man as sinner, sufferer, and saint.[1]

Children are created in the image of God, and it is the redeeming work of Christ that transforms them into saints. As image-bearers, they are born into a broken, fallen world where they are impacted by suffering and hard experiences. Young people are moral responders, at war with their sinful natures that make them prone to wander from the Lord and corrupt the ways they experience and interpret life.

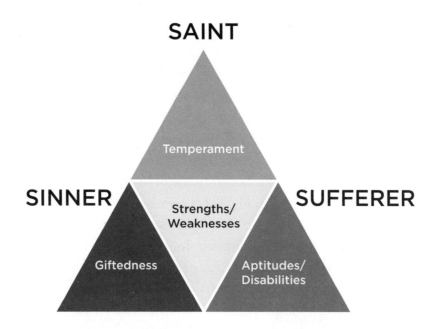

Our task is to help young people see life and their experiences from a biblical worldview. God creates, but the world corrupts. God made food, love, sex, relationships, pleasure, and our temperaments, but none of these factors is immune from being corrupted when we are not walking in submission to Christ. Good counseling and personal ministry require us to help young people gain insight into their own hearts and proclivities. It requires building a redemptive worldview where they can see that God created everything and everything points back to him (Psalm 19:1; John 1:3; Colossians 1:17). It calls for speaking, mentoring, and walking alongside them in whatever capacity we are given.

Children are not born blank slates. They come with innate personalities, aptitudes, giftings, tendencies, struggles, disabilities, and temptations, as well as temperamental strengths and weaknesses. We must endeavor to identify the unique mix of abilities, strengths, and weaknesses in our young counselees and consider how this informs the way we approach and guide them. Knowing children well gives us insight into their spiritual needs, helps us understand what motivates their behavior, and provides direction toward how to disciple them well.

Without this approach, we tend to revert to either our own natural style of relating (good or bad), assuming everyone interacts the same way, or we turn to other unbiblical approaches/methods/formulas. We look around to see "what works," and embrace methods that may seemingly produce results but lead away from pointing people to Christ.

REDEEMING THE WHOLE INDIVIDUAL IN CHRIST

The ability for adults to speak redemptively, and to accurately make sense of a child's experiences and struggles, is crucial. We want every part of a child's life to be understood in light of the gospel. We must aspire to always help kids see both who they are and what they experience in light of a biblical worldview. Regardless of the struggles or brokenness children and teens wrestle with, we want to infuse confidence in a loving Creator who knows them by name, sees their every thought, and knows the number of their days. When children learn to find identity in Christ, it creates a grid through which they can make accurate sense of hard things.

The diagram on the next page highlights how we are all made in the image of God, created to reflect his likeness. We all are impacted by sin and wrestle with a fallen nature, and are in need of redemption through Christ's work on the cross. We are also influenced by creational traits—our physical strengths and weaknesses, likes and dislikes, personality types, communication styles, and more.

To be an image-bearer means that we are created in God's likeness. We are made to magnify him, to reflect his glory. Every child and teen we meet is made in God's likeness, and we are called to treat them as such. This requires us to see others as God sees us.

Sinful or fallen nature means that we are all in need of the gospel—believer and unbeliever alike. The gospel equally transforms each of us, turning our hearts of stone to hearts of flesh (Ezekiel 36:26). We are all prone to wander, and it is important to understand how young people are impacted by the flesh and sinful desires.

Much like the picture of the sinner, saint, and sufferer, we are all also impacted by the suffering and brokenness of this world. Suffering can take the form of creational strengths and weaknesses. Perhaps it is a disability, whether physical or cognitive. For a young person, it may be learning disabilities, struggles with social skills, physical handicaps, or deformities. Or, it could be giftedness with amazing talent, skillfulness, or a high IQ—which although they are blessings on one level, can make it hard for others to understand or relate to. These are traits we were given at birth and are incapable of changing, but which we need to work on and perhaps compensate for. We each must wrestle with living in a broken physical body.

Then there are situational events: the impact of having a one-parent or two-parent home, being an only child or having multiple siblings, growing up in foster care or an orphanage, or coming from a family of divorce. It could be a history of being bullied or being the star athlete. It could be abuse or growing up in a happy, healthy home environment.

IMAGE-BEARER

CREATIONAL TRAITS

Physical
Strengths,
Weaknesses,
Personal
Abilities,
Limitations

Situational Events

Personal History
Experiences

Situational Events

Suffering
Blessings

Sinful or Fallen Nature

Regardless of their history, blessings, or sufferings, children must learn to accurately make sense of their experiences in light of Scripture. As counselors, we need to come alongside children and help them make sense of how these factors impact the way they see and respond to the world around them.

Without a biblical understanding of human nature, identity, and innate personalities, we tend to misperceive children's actions and motives. In any counseling relationship, we must look at both the creational (physical or developmental) as well as the spiritual factors at play in a young person's life. If we ignore the central spiritual need for faith and obedience, then sin could be excused as a personality trait. Likewise, if we ignore creational and situational factors, some struggles your counselee faces could be incorrectly suspected as sin.

Counselors and parents often wrestle with whether what they are seeing is a sin issue or a creational/temperamental strength or weakness. Much of the time it is both. Children do not know what to do with their inattention, forgetfulness, or social awkwardness (which would be a part of their physical development and creational traits), so they will often compensate in sinful or foolish ways. Perhaps a child is embarrassed by a learning disability, so she acts up in class or makes jokes to deflect feeling inadequate. Maybe a teenaged boy who is small and stutters will pick fights or become a bully to wrongly try to feel powerful or accepted.

We all deal with situational factors in our lives—personal histories, sufferings, blessings, and other impactful experiences. Those might include the loss of a parent, adoption, trauma, constant lifestyle upheaval, growing up in a large or small family, disability, or living in poverty or wealth. These experiences prejudice the way a child sees relationships, the world around them, and themselves. Left to themselves, they will try make sense out of their experiences and often do so inaccurately. A child who is adopted may wrongly conclude they are unlovable or bad. A child whose parents have divorced may think they could have prevented their parents' failed relationship if they had done something different or behaved better.

Children interpret life and experiences whether or not we talk to them about it. Often we avoid discussing topics that are heavy, complicated, or confusing, believing that children will not think about these factors if we do not bring them up. The problem is, children already are thinking, interpreting, and drawing conclusions about their lives. If we do not engage them about these topics, they will draw their own conclusions about themselves, their lives, and God without any loving guidance or a redemptive worldview.

Looking at each individual as a puzzle

Once you have your overall outline of a child in place, you can start working to understand the individual pieces to the puzzle that makes up who they are. A counseling relationship with a child is most often an investment, so keep the process in mind as you take the time to really know what makes a child tick. What motivates him, excites him, or causes him to cry? What does she dream about, what is she tempted by, and where is she naturally gifted? All of these factors will help you shine the light of Christ most effectively into his or her particular situation.

Imagine dumping out the pieces of a puzzle without having any idea what the finished picture looked like. It would feel a bit overwhelming. All of it lies before you, but the end result would not be clear right away. Early on we would begin making sense of it by putting together the obvious corners and straight sides, building a framework for what will unfold before us. Counseling is very much like this. We are slowly putting the pieces together and building a picture of the young person we are working with.

Often I start building my picture by asking the real experts of the child: the parents. Parents have spent years observing their children, and their perceptions come from thousands of little and big moments alike. Parents often express that they feel lost or confused about what is going on with their child; but when they are asked probing questions, they tend to be full of insights. Some questions I am likely to ask a parent are:

- Tell me what your child is like.
- What are his/her strengths and weaknesses?
- Where do you see him/her struggle?
- How does he/she respond to correction?
- What is he/she like around his/her peers?
- What makes him/her happy, anxious, angry, sad, etc.?
- Is he/she open about his/her feelings or closed off?
- What is he/she like in school? in church? in public?
- Does he/she show any spiritual maturity or sensitivity? How so?

We start with what we believe about human nature, sin, and individual temperaments, and this often helps us begin to grasp the outer contours of the child we are counseling. We don't yet know him or her well, but we can use these categories of human experience to begin creating a framework.

However, there are many, many "puzzle pieces" that make up the complete picture of who your counselee is, and understanding and piecing together the distinct components of his or her experience and strengths/weaknesses will take a bit of trial and error. As we get to know a child, we begin to get glimpses of why he does what he does, where he is developmentally, what his personality is like, how he is struggling, and what motivates him. As we understand all of these things, we can start putting the pieces of his puzzle together. Sometimes the pieces fit; sometimes we see later that they really did not connect at all. Only time, wisdom, and a commitment to knowing the child deeply will ensure an accurate, meaningful "knowing." This "knowing" is also dependent on the help of parents and other loving individuals in each young person's life.

Christ knows us by name. He knows our every thought, he sees past our behavior, and he knows what motivates us (1 Samuel 16:7; Psalm 139:1–24; Isaiah 43:1). We can't read children's minds and hearts, but we can be skillful in observing their behaviors; adept in reading what motivates them in various situations; proficient in seeing their gifts, weaknesses, aptitudes, fears, and insecurities; and wise in knowing how to speak hope into their experiences. We can excel at wooing them to a personal God who longs to work in and through them. It is not enough that we commit to knowing them well. We also want to help them understand themselves. We want children to know themselves wisely and know how to both live well before the face of God and recognize their greatest need is to lean deeply into him.

The Lord does not leave us to our own devices. He pursues us because he is a loving Father, a wise Counselor, and a good Shepherd. He meets us in our need, weakness, and frailty. The Lord is unwavering in his love for us. He shows compassion and is merciful and gracious. May we imitate him with a commitment to know, understand, and proactively pursue our young people.

Chapter 2

Ages and Stages: Understanding the Impact of Development

Every stone is different. No other stone exactly alike. . . . God loves variety. In odd days like these . . . people study how to be alike instead of how to be as different as they really are.

Dobry, Monica Shannon

Isaiah was a twelve-year-old boy who struggled with anxiety. He was physically small for his age, yet spiritually and emotionally mature beyond his years. He had developed a keen ability to read people's expressions and perceive attitudes—and potential criticism. He also struggled academically. Reading was difficult for him, which impacted his progress in other subjects as he grew older. Due to his small size, he was often picked on or overlooked in school. He was sensitive to this and began looking for ways to avoid situations where he might be rejected or chosen last.

Due to his developmental and academic struggles, many thought he might benefit from being held back a year in school. He looked like a ten-year-old boy, though he had the maturity and insight of a mature teenager. He enjoyed talking with adults and had made friends with older kids outside school. Yet he spent the majority of his day in a setting where he did not fit in. What would it look like to help Isaiah? What did he need?

Isaiah's parents needed help putting together Isaiah's puzzle pieces. They were trying to understand what was developmental about his struggles—what were his physical, temperamental, and academic strengths and weaknesses? What was situational about his difficulties—i.e., to what degree did difficult peers, bullying, or wrong educational decisions fit into the overall equation? Where was Isaiah struggling with poor responses: avoiding social situations, people, and places; or struggling with hypersensitivity to what others were thinking? Were any of these responses sinful or a lack of faith?

When attempting to accurately understand a struggling child and his or her situation, the sources of the problem are often not clear-cut. They can feel obscure and difficult to figure out. Sometimes one struggle appears to cause or connect to another. For example, did Isaiah's delay in physical growth lead to bullying, or did his higher level of maturity lead to being picked on? The answer is not always discernible, but applying as much wisdom as possible will help you to distinguish as many factors as possible in such a situation and give help accordingly.

Isaiah's parents consistently affirmed and nurtured the positive qualities they saw in his life, helping him to see his perceptiveness and sensitivity not as weaknesses but as God-given traits he must learn to steward. They learned that he needed compassion and patience as they addressed his anxiety, and they gave him tools to manage apprehensive moments. They consistently pointed him to the Lord as his comfort and help, praying for him and with him. They challenged him to face his anxieties and work through them, trusting that the Lord would give him what he needed in every circumstance.

In Isaiah's case, his parents knew he needed friends and support outside of school. We worked together to find him a mentor he could relate to. They got special permission to have him in an older youth group and connected him with one or two mature students they knew would embrace him.

His school situation was more difficult to figure out. Isaiah struggled academically and needed extra help, but we all recognized that moving him back a year would not be the optimal solution; it would very likely lead to more difficulty fitting in and a greater sense of discouragement. There was no easy answer. His parents tried securing special accommodations for him in the classroom and hired an after-school tutor. As a last resort, they eventually allowed him to be held back—only to have all our concerns about peer dynamics validated. Although both parents worked outside the home, they eventually pulled him out of school altogether and worked hard to develop a personalized homeschool program that fit his needs.

Isaiah's parents did the hard work of seeking to understand their son and exploring what they needed to change in his situation, versus what he had to learn to cope with. As in many counseling scenarios, they had to prayerfully wade through a series of trial and error, successes and failures, but continued to seek what was best for Isaiah and to ask the Lord for the provision to do so.

Understanding a young person's developmental strengths and challenges is a huge component of knowing the child God has placed in front of you, and it will be critical in your ability to accurately speak into his or her situation. (See also a detailed breakdown of what is typical for each age and stage in Appendix A: Sample Developmental

Charts.) Developmental anomalies often factor into the fabric of a child's challenges, and so it is best to examine these components early on. Our development as human beings includes physical, cognitive, emotional, social, and spiritual factors. Standard measurements of what is "typical" for a child or teen can help us to see when a child is delayed or gifted in particular ways and may need focused help. Tracking someone's development emotionally or socially can indicate whether the child is immature or advanced for his age. There are many good resources online, such as the Center for Disease Control and Prevention (www.cdc.gov) that provide the most up-to-date standards for healthy child/teen development. Many hospital websites also have scholarly articles and developmental charts online that you can easily access.

You often see young people who do not neatly fall into developmental categories for their age. When this happens, both the young person and her parents struggle to make sense out of her weaknesses, disabilities, or even giftedness. Children are also trying to figure out what's happening and often do not do so accurately. They want to be "normal" by fitting into their environment or hiding their differences. Young people try to compensate by imitating their peers when they need help understanding, embracing, and adapting wisely to their differences.

Most kids spend a majority of time in a school setting where they are presumed to be on the same level as those around them. For kids who are either behind or excel developmentally in any area, it can create a gap—a sense of being odd, different than, or less than those around them. This leads to all types of issues that regularly bring kids into counseling: learning disabilities, social rejection, anxiety, frustration, isolation, relational difficulties, bullying, etc.

What do we do when children are in some way developmentally behind or ahead of their peer group? We begin by seeking to understand them. We watch for patterns, evaluate what it indicates about the child, and consider how we need to address what is occurring. The child may be maturing at her own rate; she may simply like younger or older toys and games, or connect best with a younger or older peer group. Differences in development may not indicate that anything is wrong, but there may be a need to think creatively about how to meet the child's needs.

Counselors, educators, caring adults, and parents need to consider how a particular child's development affects his or her ability to function in age-appropriate settings. Sometimes we miss the fact that a child may meet many developmental milestones but fall significantly short on others, or excel beyond what is normal in still other categories. This can cause significant problems emotionally or socially when a child is forced to conform to what is considered average for their age. This was part of Isaiah's problem.

When does it help to acknowledge a child's differences and help that child know how to adapt? When are those differences reflective of something problematic (such as significantly underdeveloped social skills or academic processing issues)? When a weakness impedes daily life or relationships, adult helpers must consider what intervention is advantageous. We have to think about what resources are needed, including professional help, a different environment, special skills or services, etc. This isn't always immediately clear, but if you strive to understand the child well, over time you will gain discernment.

In Isaiah's case, it took time and much trial and error, but his parents and I became students of their son and I began to coach them toward healthy goals for him so he could thrive. We reflected on how he was uniquely created, where he was developmentally, what his needs were, and what gifts and aptitudes needed to be developed and encouraged. We all became experts at knowing Isaiah and worked to help him find his identity in who God fashioned him to be. Our goal was to help Isaiah be a godly Isaiah. We spoke into the places he struggled with fear, lack of faith, or temptation, and helped him understand his own proclivities. It required thinking outside the box and looking beyond the typical solutions a school district could offer, as well as being faithful to understand his heart and struggles well. In doing so, Isaiah's parents wisely established a plan to help him thrive.

SIN OR PERSONALITY TRAITS?

In seeking to understand and help a young person, it is prudent to ask when issues are developmental and when they are moral (sin) issues. Is a challenging behavior a result of willfulness and sinful desires, or just immaturity? Initially it is not always obvious. But with wisdom, time, and a willingness to engage with a child's struggles, clarity will often develop.

Children and teens, like adults, have hearts that are always active and dynamic. They are driven by wants, motives, desires, and agendas. There is nothing passive about how they live or how they experience the world. We see in Scripture and throughout history that because of sin, our agendas and motives have led us to try to create substitutes for God. We want to be in charge, we want to be center stage, and we want all of our desires to be fulfilled on our own timetables. We human beings are often tempted to exchange the Creator for the created thing—to establish mini-gods that serve our purposes. This is another critical component to consider when getting to know a child and seeking to understand his or her needs when they come to you for counseling.

One way of thinking about this multifaceted picture of your counselee is reflected in the diagram below.

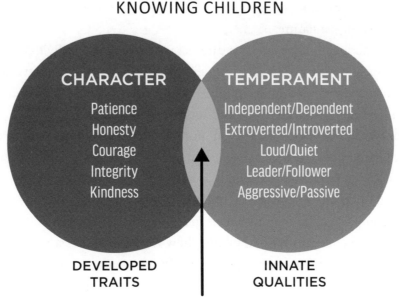

KNOWING CHILDREN

CHARACTER

Patience
Honesty
Courage
Integrity
Kindness

TEMPERAMENT

Independent/Dependent
Extroverted/Introverted
Loud/Quiet
Leader/Follower
Aggressive/Passive

DEVELOPED TRAITS

INNATE QUALITIES

Sensitivity, empathy, attentiveness,
aggressiveness, memory problems, organization

Consider the difference between character and temperament. Character is learned moral behavior; it can be sinful or godly, moral or immoral, self-serving or selfless. Temperament (strengths, weaknesses, gifting, inabilities, innate qualities and dispositions) encompasses the innate traits found in each person; we consider these to be creational in nature. They are neither sinful or godly in themselves, simply leanings in personality.

Character encompasses developed traits and moral choices regarding what and who a person will become. Temperamental attributes are innate qualities and individual tendencies a person has toward being introverted or extroverted, loud or quiet, a follower or leader, dependent or independent, organized or disorganized, etc. Children are embodied souls, with both temperament and character that need to be shaped and developed by the gospel.

Parents often wrestle with whether their child or teen is dealing with a sin issue or a physical/temperamental strength or weakness. Often it is both. Young people do not know what to do when they have difficulty paying attention, frequently forget things, or struggle with social situations, so they will often compensate in sinful ways.

Having a strong biblical framework for understanding children helps. We must look at the child as a whole, both spiritual and creational/physical. If we ignore the spiritual need for faith and obedience, sin will be excused as "this is just who [he or she] is." We can excuse sinful tendencies as if they are simply part of a strength or weakness, or we can allow temperamental wirings to become corrupted by sin and become self-serving in nature.

On the other hand, if we ignore creational weaknesses and individual differences, we turn temperamental weaknesses into character issues and discipline our children for things that are not immoral or sinful in nature. They begin to feel condemned for things that are genuine weaknesses, and ultimately will believe that God condemns them, too. We do not want to fail to call immoral behavior sin; nor things that are a result of a broken body, weakness. Even then, however, we want our children to learn greater reliance on God, whose strength is made perfect in weakness.

That said, there are times when an innate temperamental trait becomes a character issue. For example, a child might struggle greatly with attentiveness and organization (temperament). He doesn't naturally know how to organize, has a poor memory, or just doesn't know where to begin with a task. When we understand this, we do not fault him; we help him. However, when he is given skills and resources to help him and he chooses not to apply these tools, that choice becomes a sin (character) issue. The sinful choice may be motivated by laziness over the effort required, or a lack of concern for how it impacts the people around him. It could also be that he avoids attempting what feels insurmountable. No matter what the reason, the child is a moral responder in the choice he makes. The more we understand what is going on behind the behavior, the greater success we will have in speaking into the issue.

Counseling a child through this lens also means learning to contextualize Scripture to fit the child or teen before us. Formulas and ideals run aground because we assume that if we plug every child into our formulas, they will all come out as poster children for success. Instead, young people whom we attempt to help by surface formulas are often hindered or harmed. As we approach ministering to young people, it would be helpful to ask ourselves whether we are becoming discerning at knowing this child well. What does this particular child need?

Perhaps what we must grapple with is the need for wisdom in drawing out young people. There is both wisdom and skill in weeding through what is characterological or behavioral in nature, versus innate weaknesses or developmental traits that produce difficulties but are not sinful in nature. When does something simply require more maturity yet is appropriate for the developmental stage a child is in, and when should a parent or adult be concerned by a child's behavior?

There are some situations that are fairly straightforward. A child is acting out in school due to anxiety, jealousy, or family dynamics at home. We address it, replace what motivates the behavior, and we see change. There are other situations where complexity abounds. A child has poor behavior, is acting out sinfully, is being mistreated, has learning difficulties, or is falling behind in school and feels rejected. Where do we begin helping such a child? These are the situations we must become more discerning and adept at tackling.

Let's consider another scenario. Billy is a nine-year-old boy. Billy is stronger and bigger than most boys his age; he looks more like a twelve-year-old. Billy is energetic, strong, and aggressive with kids at school. He likes to boast about how good he is at most everything. His bravado is a cover for the fact that he is really struggling academically. He is below grade level in math and reading and performs poorly academically. He feels insecure and dumb so he tries to compensate by fitting in with the tough boys. He doesn't pay attention to instruction and covers for his struggles by acting bored or being disruptive in class. His emotional development seems to be behind; he seems to be either unaware or unconcerned about how his actions impact those around him.

At home, Billy plays with miniature dinosaurs, often acting out his social struggles through his play. Billy is from a divorced family. He lives with his mother, visiting his father on weekends. His father is an alcoholic who uses intimidation as a form of parenting. His mother works long hours and feels overwhelmed by Billy's needs.

Billy is a puzzle, and a caring adult or counselor will need wisdom to know what pieces fit together and how to understand what he needs to thrive. He does not fall neatly into a developmental chart, nor does he struggle only with behavioral issues or sinful tendencies, nor can we chalk everything up to a disability. His family situation impacts him, but this too does not explain all his struggles. How will we make sense of what is going on in this young boy's life, and where do we begin ministering to him?

As mentioned before, sometimes when a child is either delayed or even advanced in a particular area of development, it can cause challenges that impair his or her growth or relationships. Children may feel odd or different than their peers when they do not have shared developmental experiences. This is true of Billy. He is struggling academically and is behind in class. The disconnect between his advanced physical development and his emotional and academic deficit create a chasm of frustration and struggle with his peer group. Add to this struggle the pain of a fractured family and a hard relationship with his father. Billy and his mother need someone to come alongside them and help Billy make sense of his world and learn to move forward in a healthy way.

As we develop our ability to recognize developmental issues and character/behavioral choices, we will become wiser at understanding both the problems and the solutions. We can help bring light and resources to the places where one is weak, and rightly confront and challenge growth in the places where one needs to give up their personal agenda to conform to Christ.

DEVELOPMENT

It is important for us to think through how the child's development may be playing into child/teen's immediate struggles. Skilled professionals such as doctors, educators, and learning specialists also rely on knowing what is within normal, healthy development in order to identify where specific problems lie. The more knowledgeable we are of developmental capabilities in children and teens, the better we become at discerning what an individual can or should be capable of doing. Such understanding helps shape what we should expect in terms of goals or growth at any age. It also helps us to identify when a young person seems to fall significantly outside what is normal for his age and to ask how this might be influencing him.

There are many models of development that those who work with youth follow. For the purpose of one-on-one ministry, a sample of stages and their characteristics has been provided in Appendix A. Each stage has general milestones that provide a sense of where a child might fall, but there is always a spectrum that gives room for various rates of development. The charts are not meant to be exhaustive but serve as an example to help you consider how to approach ministry for each particular age group.

It is essential to become an expert at knowing the child in front of you. You must wisely evaluate the child's development and if (or how) it might be impacting her. You must distinguish where she is maturing but at a slower rate, or where she may be excelling but still within a normal range. You must evaluate when she surpasses her age in certain areas of development or where she may be significantly behind in ways that are detrimental and require intervention.

As we observe lifestyles, cultural norms, and patterns, we will also see changes in how children develop. For example, some research shows that children who spend more time on electronic devices are often slower in developing hand strength; because of this, their ability to hold pencils, cut with scissors, string beads, color, or work with puzzles is significantly delayed. Things such as this are not always reflected in developmental guidelines but do impact where children's functioning is affected by social norms.

Why is this important for those who counsel or minister to youth? Because developmental accelerations or delays often have emotional, social, and spiritual implications for young people. It impacts how they view themselves, compare themselves to others, or make sense out of their experiences. We must be prepared to help them navigate such things accurately.

For example, if a child is very concrete in his thinking, we will confuse him with metaphors and analogies he cannot comprehend. We tend to see this in young children, in kids on the autism spectrum, and even in teenagers who are just quite literal and concrete in nature. We can frustrate them, and ourselves, by attempting to make them be abstract when they are incapable.

Likewise, if a child has a short attention span but we force her to sit, talk, and focus for longer than is loving, we create frustration, an unpleasant atmosphere, and a resistance in her to return or engage with us. It is likely we will blame the child—she is simply undisciplined or stubborn (and at times this may be true). However, there are times when it has much more to do with the rigidity of our approach than it does the willingness of the young person.

There are children who feel intimidated by direct eye contact and who would open up much more quickly if we provided a distraction (such as an activity, or simply drawing or building something) while talking. They engage with less effort and more vulnerability when given something to do with their hands. Activities that draw young people out can be very useful and fruitful; this will be discussed further in Chapter 4.

Our knowledge of children must also inform how we approach them and engage in conversation. Ministering to and speaking into the lives of young people requires us to do our best to make our words as winsome, clear, and attractive to them as possible. I often see children and teens who are weak in processing information. If we do not adapt our interactions, we lose them in conversation. They miss what we are saying. They don't want to look foolish, so they don't ask. Instead, they tune us out—and we write them off as unwilling or rebellious, when in reality they simply don't comprehend what we're telling them. The responsibility is on us to find open doors into their world, and to both draw them out and speak back in effectively.

It is particularly important for those ministering to kids/teens to grasp how they understand, learn, process, and solve problems. It is easy to assume that they should think like us, know things we know, or have a wealth of examples and information to draw from. When children do not understand, they will often just nod their heads or let us continue talking at them. If we are fortunate, a young person will actually tell us they don't understand; but for the most part, many simply placate us.

Some studies even suggest that young people's brains do not fully develop or "grow up" until well into their late twenties.[2] Though physically a young person may look and even talk in a mature way, we know they often struggle emotionally, socially, and spiritually. They are wrestling to make sense out of their experiences. They need loving, wise adults in their lives helping to guide them, know them, and speak into their experiences. Kids are not fixed in development; they are a work in progress. This means we must be constantly reevaluating where they are at and how we can contribute to their growth.

What a six-year-old girl and a thirteen-year-old girl are going through cognitively will be very different (we hope). Where a seven-year-old boy and a fifteen-year-old boy are emotionally will be very different. Regardless of the counseling issue or need in a young person's life, it is important that we consider where he or she is developmentally; this includes physical, cognitive, emotional, social, and spiritual factors. Then, we must consider how where they are developmentally shapes how we will engage them.

As mentioned earlier in this chapter, there are many good resources to consult about typical development in kids and teens, as well as developmental charts you can look up to better understand where a child may fall at his or her stage of life. These can help you evaluate whether your expectations of a child's behavior, understanding, and overall development are realistic, and give indication to where there might be weakness or deficits developmentally. It can also give you insight as to why they might be struggling and how you can help them grow. But again, remember that children don't always fall into neat developmental categories.

I do not believe development directs everything we do; it simply helps build a bigger, better picture of the child as a whole. Development, temperament, and innate traits and characteristics are not determinative in a person's life. It is imperative that our observations are informed by a biblical worldview—one that views young people as image-bearers, understands human nature, and acknowledges our inherent bent toward sin and how our bodies and development are impacted by sin and weakness, suffering and brokenness.

As children and teens develop, they are forming views of identity, self-understanding, normalcy and values, relationships (with man and God), and moral decision-making. We also know that we all process life and our experiences differently, and often inaccurately. Children need wisdom outside themselves; they need help understanding who they are before the Lord, and how to live in a broken world. When they look or feel different than peers, when they cannot keep up with those around them, or when they are not accepted for their differences, we need to point them to a Creator who helps make sense of their experiences.

Learning to understand both development and the nature of the human heart will help you develop wisdom in putting the pieces of the puzzle together to help young people.

Chapter 3

The Importance of Involving Parents

Bill and Amanda are the parents of three children: Matthew (age four), Rachel (age six), and Micah (age fourteen). They both work outside the home, are regularly involved in church, and are trying their best to juggle the busyness of life and family activities. Like many parents, they are looking for solutions to the problems that their children are experiencing. Micah is consumed with his phone and seems to be slowly withdrawing from family life. Rachel is anxious and struggles just to get on the morning bus, and Matthew is a typical high-energy child who wears his mother out with his constant movement.

Bill and Amanda came for counseling to find out what they could do to make their family "function normally." As we talked together about what "normal function" meant to them, we realized that they were looking for "*the* thing" they could do so that their kids would obey, not struggle, and be happy, decent young people. Surely there was *a* right thing—a foolproof recipe for producing the results they were looking for?

You and I can understand this mentality. We want relationships where we can sit down and reason with others about their behavior and choices and win them over with our insight. This is not a bad ideal. However, parents mistakenly believe that there is one way that is best for their children, which may or may not be true.

There are many times in counseling when it is the parents who need help to know how to navigate the struggles of their children. When this is the case, we want to make sure we are helping parents change and grow to love and shepherd their children in increasingly wise and helpful ways.

As a counselor, my goal is to work myself out of a job. I enter into a young person's life for a season, to come alongside and aid their process of change and growth. Parents are invested into the lives of their children for the long term. Therefore, it makes sense that when we are working with children and teens, we must always to some degree be working to equip parents, their primary mentors.

It is concerning to me how often parents are left out of the counseling process for their child or teen, regardless of the young person's age. Too many counselors perceive parents as a hindrance or stumbling block to working with kids. Sometimes a counselor's reluctance is because the presence of parents in the room hinders children from opening up. Other times, it is because parents can take over the discussion and answer for their child. Inadvertently, a parent may have a different agenda and work against what a counselor may be trying to accomplish. These complications can certainly happen, which is why it is important for us as counselors to discuss expectations and goals with parents ahead of time.

It would be easy to continue to list the many reasons why it may be challenging to have parents as part of their child's counseling process. However, I believe a biblical understanding of family mandates us to see parents as their child's primary counselors, mentors, instructors, and disciplers (Deuteronomy 11:19; Psalm 78:5–7; Proverbs 22:6). Culturally, our society is moving away from this idea, believing that we should leave this nurturing work to the "experts." We forget that God has placed parents in the position of being their child's experts. Parents struggle more and more with helping their children with the tough things they are facing, Whether it is rapidly changing social norms, the pace of life families are trying to maintain, or the emphasis on peer culture, young people are missing the influence of mature, godly adults. All the more reason, then, that parents should be vital participants in the counseling process.[3]

I often tell parents that no one will be as committed to knowing their child as they are. Counselors, mentors, and other professionals have important observations to make and insights to share, but their knowledge usually pales in comparison to what a parent will know about his or her child. Parents who are committed to understanding their kids will tend to know things that seem intuitive but actually come from years of watching, listening, observing, and interacting with their children.

This is not to say that parental involvement will look the same in every counseling situation. Many factors—the age of the child, the quality of the parent/child relationship, and the child's particular struggle—will determine the most beneficial arrangement. There will be situations where parents can't be involved at all due to abuse, safety issues, abandonment, foster care, and the like. In those cases, consider if there are other caring adults who may be a support in the process. There are many other circumstances that call for a parent to be actively involved in meetings and discussions, such as situations that require intervention: eating disorders, suicide, academic challenges, and crisis. Even when there is no crisis, we know that kids can only control so much of what goes on in their world and are still reliant on parents and a family. It is always beneficial to include family when possible. In most cases, familiarizing ourselves with a particular young person's situation will inform when and how to bring the parent into the discussion, and there is a lot of flexibility in how this can be done.

For many counselors, the younger the child is, often the more it is necessary to involve parents. Young children often lack the ability to make good decisions for themselves and lack the resources to change. In these instances, parental action is often the key to helping a child overcome his or her struggles. Some children's issues may need to be addressed directly with the parent instead of with the child. A counselor can provide insight, guidance, and resources to the parent, who then returns home and works to incorporate these strategies.

It is equally valuable to have parental involvement as children get older, though it may look different. Although it feels easier to directly engage with older children and teens and to gain insight into their situation, it does not minimize the need to engage their parents. Teens are becoming more and more disconnected from their parents and more connected to their peers. It is increasingly valuable for counselors to look for ways to help build connections between parents and teens. Just as trust is important for us as counselors to build bridges of credibility with a teen, we also want to facilitate that bond between teens and their parents.

I will often share with teens that as much time and attention that I give to working with them, I want to work at the same level with their parents in order to help their parents know how to love them better. Rarely will a teen say no to that. If they do, it reveals a considerable barrier to be addressed.

Sometimes parents are indeed part of the problem, and the parent/child dynamic becomes the focus of change. However, whether parents are part of the problem or not, they must always be part of the solution. This means we involve them in the initial data-gathering; we ask them about their goals for counseling, and we gather as much information as possible about their child and their concerns. We then share our philosophy of counseling and allow them to ask questions to make sure the arrangement is a good fit. It is far better to find out whether or not we are on the same page as the parents before we meet with their child.

Often parents want an immediate solution to their problems—when what they really need is time to learn and understand their child and what factors have contributed to the challenges at hand. They need time to examine their child individually, to prayerfully ask what it looks like to help him or her, and then to make informed decisions for the benefit of their child. Parents need encouragement. They will not always get it right, but when they are committed to knowing and loving their child well, they can trust God with the outcome. It does not mean that the counseling will go smoothly or that the best direction will always be clear from the beginning. However, we can help parents find hope, and support them in being faithful to the task God has given them.

Family to family, the needs and struggles of children and teens vary. Consider the following differences I have observed in children I have counseled:

- Some children argue or are oppositional/defiant. They need structure and accountability.
- Some children nod their heads yes while silently disagreeing. They need someone to notice and gently call them out.
- Some children are sensitive and have a tendency to withdraw. They lack self-awareness and need a patient adult who will draw them out and reflect back to them.
- Some children demonstrate developmental delays or impairments that impact how they hear or process information. They need a tailor-made approach to their challenges that will help them learn.
- Some children do not respond to laid-back parenting; they thrive on routines and rhythms. They need to be highly structured and disciplined or they fall into unhealthy or ungodly patterns.
- Some children do not respond well to overly structured households; they need grace and extra time, and less pressure to think and accomplish tasks.

In this list, each indicated parental response is based on the needs of the individual child instead of the parent's (or counselor's) preferences. A parent's knowledge of a child can and should shape how they shepherd them; engage with their struggles and weaknesses; address the temptations and sin that entices them; and encourage their strengths, gifting, and spiritual sensitivity. Therefore, we always want to help parents engage well, and wisely.

Parents are perfectly positioned for this task. Although outside help and professionals are an aid and often necessary, we want parents to know that they are the experts. This means that they likely know their children best, and when committed to putting aside their preferences to really evaluate the needs of their children, they become the experts. Very few people in a child's life will be as committed to knowing and understanding that child as his or her parents. They spend the most time and energy with the child. They have more conversations and share more everyday life with their children than anyone else. Often they can intuitively read their faces, body language, and silences. They sense when something is amiss.

One of our kids always gets a "caught look" when he does something wrong. His face always gives it away when he is lying. Thankfully he has never figured out what that look is. Not all kids are so obvious, but parents can still pick up on subtle cues.

We develop this sensitivity as counselors as well. Instinct and experience kick in and tell us the child we are talking to is hiding something, or hurting, or acting out of character. When a teenager comes in and does not make eye contact, says her day was fine, but is clearly emotional and more withdrawn than you've seen her, it is a signal that things are askew.

It means that we notice, pay attention, and pursue her. When she shuts down conversation, we or a parent notice and pursue it or file away the moment in hopes the Lord will provide insight or opportunity to address it at a later time. For example, a teen gets choked up when talking about a painful situation at school, yet he claims "I don't care" or "It was no big deal." The teen comes home and downplays it, but the parent notices he is emotional, withdrawn, and hurting. As time goes on, the parent senses more is going on and struggles to know what to do. They are often correctly picking up on a child's problems. Uncertain if they are overreacting or underreacting, they need affirmation about what they are discerning and help to know how to proceed.

Parents know their children in ways that would take a professional counselor months to figure out. Parents can predict reactions from their children and can discern when they are not acting like themselves. To have parents as part of the process can save us as counselors valuable time and energy as we get to know the child or teen we are working with. Sometimes we just need to help parents slow down enough to evaluate and piece together what they know and perceive.

As a counselor, when I talk through circumstances with parents, I often find that their perceptions are accurate. Many parents question their instincts, wonder why they feel strongly about something, and wonder if they are wrong. Probably any parent or counselor should be open to asking those questions. However, as I draw out why they feel a certain way, often facts and details emerge that support their conclusion. They've just never taken the time to untangle their thoughts and perceptions. We need to respect and support the reality that God has put parents in the unique position of being their child's wisest counselors. They have years of experience and interactions that shape what they know.

Of course, parents are at times wrong, blind to dynamics in their child's life, misperceive their motives, or can be driven by their own sinful reactions. Having Mom and Dad included in the counseling process will help unearth when this is happening and provide an opportunity to address it. Parents sometimes need an outside perspective to see what they are too close to see. A counselor can give fresh perspective and objective input, and can help equip parents with understanding so that they can parent wisely.

Parents can mistakenly believe their child's struggles must be a result of something they are doing wrong. If they were good parents, their kids wouldn't struggle, right?

We can encourage parents that sometimes children go through hard things that have nothing to do with good or bad parenting, but do require a response. Parents need guidance in figuring out how to help their child through the difficult things they are facing.

As biblical counselors, we have the best foundation for guiding parents. We have the Scripture, which is useful for reproof, correction, and training (2 Timothy 3:16). The Bible does not always give us specifics on how to help a child in the midst of a temper tantrum, or what to do when a teen struggles with pornography. But it does give us the principles for responding and parenting well (discipleship, discipline, stewardship, guidance, and training). As we ask, the Spirit gives us all wisdom to apply general principles to the specifics of a child's life.

God's Word gives counselors and parents alike the wisdom to know how to engage relationally with young people and carefully walk through moments of suffering, defiance, anger, grief, anxiety, and discipline. God's Word gives us the encouragement to persevere in faithfulness and prayer for children. Within that framework, there is specific guidance for every interaction and the help of the Spirit to apply the right principle at the right time.

ENCOURAGING PROACTIVE INSTEAD OF REACTIVE PARENTING

When a child or teen comes to counseling, it is usually in response to some type of struggle, problem, or behavior in the child's life. Parents rarely bring kids to counseling proactively—meaning, they identify a significant pattern in the child's life before they decide it has become urgent and seek outside input and encouragement. When this happens, it may look and feel more like mentoring or discipleship.

Too often parents respond reactively rather than proactively to their children. They wait to have a hard conversation until a child is in trouble. Perhaps a child has a relatively minor struggle like not brushing her teeth, hiding her homework, and/or arguing with her siblings. Or perhaps the problems have escalated to cheating in school, fighting at recess, using inappropriate apps or websites, pornography, sexting, sexually acting out, and/or using drugs. Either way, parents often tend to wait too long to speak into a child's life. Parents need help being prepared to offer their children biblical guidance when they first notice their children deep in a struggle or sin pattern.

This is how Charles Spurgeon explained the difference between proactive and reactive parenting:

I heard of a man who said that he did not like to prejudice his boy, so he would not say anything to him about Religion. The devil, however, was quite willing to prejudice the lad, so very early in life he learned to swear, although his father had a foolish and wicked objection to teaching him to pray. If ever you feel it incumbent upon you not to prejudice a piece of ground by sowing good seed on it, you may rest assured that the weeds will not imitate your impartiality. Where the plow does not go and the seed is not sown, the weeds are sure to multiply. And if children are left untrained, all sorts of evil will spring up in their hearts and lives.[4]

Spurgeon's point was that it is better to proactively shape our child's view on a subject than to try to debunk or uproot an inaccurate view. It is far better to teach them God's way of living than to wait to speak up until they have gone their own (wrong) way. Kids need a biblical view of life and the world around them—one that extends to every area of their lives and every issue they might face. If parents don't share a biblical perspective with them, someone else will share their worldview and it may not line up at all with truth. The more parents proactively bring their children to God's Word, while engaging in their world, the more they will equip their young people to stand up against the temptations and pressures they face.

When adults remain silent, children will perceive their silence either as indifference, inadequacy, or both. As counselors, we have to be committed to knowing what temptations children face in their school, peer groups, and social media, and then be willing to not only engage all of these issues with them but also to teach and encourage parents to do so as well.

Working with young people means also helping parents. Teaching proactive parenting means always paying attention to the subtle patterns that tend to creep into children's lives or a family's lifestyle. Practices that don't seem problematic at first and may even be necessary (such as skipping family dinnertime or allowing kids to be occupied by electronics) slowly become habits and gradually change the dynamics in the home. These less-than-healthy patterns eventually erode relationships and meaningful connection with children.

As counselors, we need to be alert to how passive parenting has affected the homes of the families we are counseling. As I interact with families, I am often concerned that there is more and more passivity entering into modern-day parenting. Although I am sure this phenomenon is not entirely new, I notice that parents today often desire to occupy kids rather than engage them. Much of the time they are trying to keep the children busy and involved in an endless stream of activity, while also maintaining their own busy schedules. Added to this is the overuse of electronics that makes it easy for kids to be occupied for large periods of time. Some parents feel that electronic devices are safe in-home babysitters. It might feel like the children are safer; after all, when they are using an electronic device they can be home, occupied, and in close proximity to their parents. Parents can see them, know what they are doing (they presume), and feel good that they are spending time at home.

As we counsel parents, it's good for us to remember that every parent has times when he or she just needs a little peace and quiet—a half hour or so where the kids are engaged in a game or watching TV—so that they can finish a project or cook dinner. These are not the moments to be concerned about. The real concern lies in the endless hours spent surfing the internet, watching videos, living on social media, and a routine of coming home from school and spending the majority of "family time" in separate rooms engaged in another world. Even if the whole family is home, there is little interaction, no meaningful conversation, and everyone is essentially living in their own world within the same walls.

Parents are tempted to allow this—it is easier than direct engagement and seems benign—but this is not proactive parenting. Instead of getting to know children, parents who allow this disconnect are letting them drift away. Instead of active relationship building and teaching biblical principles that will help their children live kindly and wisely, parents who aren't on their guard can end up allowing their children to live in a world of their own where most of their direct input is from their peers or some form of media.

Kids may come into counseling for one presenting problem when it is not actually the primary issue. I am finding more and more that kids are wrestling with these things as secondary issues. For example, a parent brings a fifteen-year-old son to counseling because his grades have dropped, he is in danger of getting kicked off his baseball team, and he just got caught sexting his girlfriend; these are the primary reasons he is in counseling. However, as you begin to dig deeper, you find out he feels disconnected from his family, his peers are becoming his voice of reason and wisdom, and his parents have lost the ability have a voice/influence in his life. It is impossible to address such things well without parenting entering into the equation. Parents may or may not be part of the problem, but they are always going to be part of the solution.

As counselors, we can be of particular blessing and support when we invite parents directly into the process of ministering to their children. Although we may primarily be working one-on-one with a young person, we need to keep in the forefront of our minds that parents need encouragement and guidance as well. We are being entrusted with the parents' most precious charge. They will take their child home each day and will need our support to steer through troubled waters. Let's not forget to make them a part of the process of helping their children.

Chapter 4

Expressive Activities: A Biblical Rationale

The purpose in a man's heart is like deep water, but a man of understanding will draw it out.

(Proverbs 20:5)

Far too often, we expect children and teens to be insightful and articulate. We expect them to tell us what they are thinking and feeling, and then tell us why. This level of self-awareness is too much to expect even of some adults. As counselors, we need to work hard to gain wisdom and skills that will help draw out the inner world of an individual. We want to be winsome, prudent, and thoughtful in the way we help uncover what is going on deep inside a person.

Children are usually not at a developmental stage where they can self-reflect. They often do not have the capacity, maturity, or skills to think about their emotions, thought processes, and motivations. They *have* emotions, thoughts, and are very much motivated by internal desires but are often at a loss to understand these dynamics themselves, yet alone verbalize them to us.

Young people are always expressing their hearts, whether they realize it or not. In counseling we want to provide a natural means for them to express what is happening internally. This practice requires us, as Proverbs 20:5 states above, to grow in the skill of engaging and drawing them out. We also then are to strive to be equally skilled and endearing in speaking truth into their lives. Colossians 4:6 encourages us in this practice: "Let your speech always be gracious, seasoned with salt, so that you may know how you ought to answer each person."

As mentioned earlier, much of our success or failure at drawing out children has more to do with our skill in connecting with them than their ability to articulate themselves. We should be very careful to be quick to listen and slow to speak (James 1:19) as we get to know a young person. Our efforts to know and understand a child are vital to moving forward in a way that accurately and personally meets the child at his or her point of need. The methods below provide direct avenues to open up this type of constructive dialogue.

WHAT WE MEAN BY "EXPRESSIVE ACTIVITIES"

I am partial to using the term *expressive therapies* or *expressive activities* to describe my methods of helping draw out the inner world of my young counselees, because this concept encompasses many methods and expressive outlets that I have found to be particularly helpful.

Expressive activities are demonstrative, winsome ways to draw out what is going on in the heart and mind of an individual. Each activity is both expressive (meaningful and communicative) and projective (symbolic of their inner world) and seeks to find ways to understand individuals and help them grow. The activities are used to help uncover a person's thoughts and feelings in a nonthreatening, indirect fashion. They are avenues toward meeting a child on his or her level developmentally and emotionally. As we use them, we enter into a young person's world and experiences using methods most natural for them. We step outside of our own natural way of relating to children and use their "language" to enter into their world.

Consider how Anne Sullivan, a tutor, reached into the darkness and confusion of young Helen Keller's world. Helen, who had been blind and deaf since infancy, was considered unreachable. She had frequent violent and uncontrollable outbursts due her inability to communicate with those around her. Her world was dark, lonely, and seemingly inaccessible, until Anne Sullivan entered into her life and endeavored to break through her silence. A battle ensued to reach the seemingly unreachable—Helen's mind and heart. *The Miracle Worker* is the story of a tutor's love, determination, and persistence to break down the barriers and darkness of Helen Keller's world. Helen had no language or means for expressing herself or her world. Her teacher gave her a means for expressing what was inside of her—a language to draw her out. Sheer commitment and dedication led Anne to use hand signs and objects to enter Helen's dark and silent experience and breathe in life and hope.[5]

That's the kind of incarnate love that God is calling us to exhibit to the children who come to us for help. It's the kind of love that meets people where they are, then encourages them to grow in love toward God and others.

Think of the many ways God modeled this manner of love to us. We understand God only because he reached down and engaged us on our level. He spoke to us in ways we could understand, using stories and parables, creation, and more to communicate who he is and who we are in relation to him (Psalm 19:1–4; Romans 1:19–20). He did even more than that by sending his Son to fully live out our experience and dwell among us, ultimately dying on the cross for us (Philippians 2:6–8). Jesus fully entered into our brokenness and humanity, our limitations and struggles (Hebrews 4:15). He entered into our dark experience and breathed in life and hope.

Missionaries understand this as well—the need to fully immerse themselves into a culture, a language, and a mindset to really know, understand, and minister to an unreached people group. It takes time, energy, resources, and careful study to know how a different culture operates, thinks, and approaches life, as well as how to determine how to effectively bring the gospel to them.

Think of other populations who struggle to express what is going on internally: the mentally or physically disabled, those with brain injuries, the elderly, etc. There are many people who find themselves in a stage of life or a situation where they no longer have the verbal skills to communicate with the world around them. They are trapped, with no way to convey their needs or desires. The love of God compels us to be thoughtful, intentional, and winsome in engaging people well. It is our responsibility and privilege to find ways to engage with children and teens.

EXPRESSIVE ACTIVITIES IN COUNSELING

Perhaps you've heard of expressive activities and expressive therapies before. You have a vague awareness that they are often used in the counseling practice to help all clients, but particularly young people. Let's take a look at how these methods are often used in the therapeutic field. Consider the following picture:

THE UMBRELLA OF EXPRESSIVE THERAPIES

Play Therapy
Drama Therapy
Dance Therapy
Bibliotherapy

Art Therapy
Animal-Assisted Therapy
Music Therapy
Sand Tray Therapy
Additional Therapies

Most often, art, drama, dance, music, animals, and other tactile experiences are used in the world of play therapy (a term I will define below). I will attempt to broaden the language of play therapy to include (and transform) those activities into something more expressive or "creational."

The Association for Play Therapy (APT) defines play therapy as "the systematic use of a theoretical model to establish an interpersonal process wherein trained play therapists use the therapeutic powers of play to help clients prevent or resolve psychosocial difficulties and achieve optimal growth and development."[6]

Because of its name, many people who hear the term "play therapy" mistakenly assume a counselor is just sitting with a child, playing with toys, and that there is very little intentional work being done. When a counselor is committed to really helping a young person grow and heal, this couldn't be further from the truth. There is skillfulness in knowing how to use play to draw out a young person and thoughtfully speak back into his or her world.

Those in the (secular) play-therapy field work hard to speak the language of children. They work to find tools and resources that help children resolve life struggles. There is a commitment to understanding children developmentally, having a knowledge of the issues young people face, understanding the impact of those painful events, and offering resources to help children heal and grow. Some very brief descriptions of these therapies are as follows:

- Art Therapy: the use of visual arts (painting, coloring, collaging, sculpting, drawing, etc.) to allow for creative expression and help express struggles and overcome the limitations of language. If emotions are too difficult, confusing, or painful to be verbalized, art can become another avenue for working through hard things.

- Animal-Assisted Therapy: a counseling intervention that incorporates animals (horses, dogs, cats, pigs, birds, etc.) into counseling in order to increase or complement the benefits of counseling. More than simply spending time with an animal, animal-assisted therapy involves specific goals, plans, and results. This therapy is often used in court proceedings, nursing homes, schools, libraries, etc.

- Bibliotherapy: Sometimes referred to as poetry therapy or therapeutic storytelling, it is a creative-arts approach that incorporates storytelling or the reading of specific texts with a healing purpose.

- Sandplay Therapy: a nonverbal intervention using a sandbox, toy figures, and sometimes water to create miniature worlds reflecting one's inner thoughts, struggles, and concerns.

- Music Therapy: The therapeutic use of music or musical activities that typically involves listening to music, singing, playing musical instruments, or composing music to bring about a certain outcome. This is often used in various populations; for example, nursing homes will often incorporate harpists, and other forms of music therapy, to minister to that population.
- Horticultural Therapy: the use of gardening or plant-based activities, facilitated by a trained counselor to accomplish specific therapeutic therapy goals.

This list isn't meant to be exhaustive, but to give a picture of methodologies that can be used to help facilitate interpersonal communication, reduce anxiety, improve cognitive functioning, promote physical rehabilitation, or resolve life's struggles.

Many in the professional counseling field believe that only licensed professionals can use play therapeutically to help individuals better articulate themselves and solve their problems. This is like saying that playing with kids helps, but don't try this at home—only a trained professional can do this! While there is always wisdom in developing a professionally practiced way of understanding and helping others, often the secular world takes many things that you and I know to be relationally wise and helpful, and turns them into a therapeutic model that only experts can access.

METHODOLOGY AND WORLDVIEW

As counselors who follow the Lord and whose practice is grounded in his Word, we understand that no counseling method is neutral in its approach to people. All therapies and methodologies come with presuppositions and philosophical underpinnings that inform how techniques are used. We must always work to discern what is behind any method before embracing it. Sometimes secular therapies work *despite*, not because of, their philosophical understanding. We should never adopt counseling methods uncritically, but ask ourselves how each one fits into God's world and his ways.

Many mainstream counseling methods have been developed apart from a distinctly Christian worldview, so naturally when we examine them, we will find the potential for faulty presuppositions and wrong conclusions about people and their problems. However, this does not mean these methods cannot be helpfully incorporated into counseling in ways that are distinctly Christian and biblical. Expressive therapies can work, but for much richer, deeper, more accurate reasons when we reinterpret them through a biblical grid.

Because the love of God calls us to move toward others and understand them, to varying degrees we all need to work at winsomely drawing out each other. While staying committed to being biblically wise in our understanding of human nature, we can benefit from the insights these methods provide in our endeavors to draw others out.

What the world tries to makes sense of, Scripture explains better. Creation reorients us to the Creator, and all beauty is meant to point us to the Master Artist. The vastness of God's world puts the temporal nature of our problems and life into full focus. It relaxes us, frees us, and reminds us what is of value. Keeping this in mind, we realize that in God's grace he has provided many ordinary experiences in this world to give reflective, restorative opportunities for personal reflection. Expressive activities can help us experience God's grace and healing through ordinary activities.

Consider the following questions:

- Why can a veteran with PTSD feel calm and more at peace kayaking down a river?
- Why do people go on walks or hikes to clear their mind?
- Why is it soothing to pet a horse or hold an animal? Why do we feel a little less alone?
- Why do we long to sit on a beach with our feet in the sand and our face in the air and watch the waves, the vastness of the ocean—and why does this tend to help put life back in perspective?
- Why do children enjoy sandboxes and building sandcastles on the beach?
- What is it about digging in the dirt and planting something beautiful that feels life-giving and fulfilling?
- Why do nursing homes, hospitals, and even courts find that having an animal present brings life, delight, and comfort to the disheartened?

Animal-assisted therapy, nature-assisted therapy, wilderness therapy, horticultural therapy, sandplay therapy, music therapy, and other forms of play therapy all tap into a truth that creation offers something healing and reorienting in our lives. There are many examples of how nature and creation minister to us.

Nature points to a very personal Creator. Creation refocuses us. It points to Someone much greater than ourselves and woos us into relationship with him—one who is personal and interactive, not passive and distant. Creation inherently points us to the God who is bigger than ourselves and our struggles. Psalm 19:1–2 expresses this beautifully: "The heavens declare the glory of God, and the sky above proclaims his handiwork. Day to day pours out speech, and night to night reveals knowledge."

I like to think of expressive therapy as "creational counseling"—using things in nature to remind us of biblical truths and point us to the Lord. It would seem both winsome and wise to use his creation to woo those we counsel to what is true, right, and good. We are taking the things that the world has secularized or "therapeutized," and reclaiming what is biblical and life-giving about our experience with nature.

Kyle was a fourteen-year-old boy who did not want to be in counseling. Like many young people, he was coming because his parents wanted him to, not because he admitted he needed help. His parents saw a noticeable change in his demeanor toward school, as well as toward his family. He was less tolerant, easily agitated, and his grades were quickly slipping. In the last month Kyle had been sent to the principal's office twice, refusing to cooperate in class and showing disrespect toward a teacher. In my initial session with the parents, they warned me he may be hostile in the first session.

When I greeted Kyle with a smile and introduced myself, Kyle did not respond. He simply stood up and followed me as though he were headed for the guillotine. I asked, "Kyle, do you like dogs? I have a therapy dog in my office; would that be OK with you?"

Already aware from his parents that Kyle did indeed like dogs, I waited to see how he'd respond. He shrugged without looking up, but as soon as I opened my office door a smile crossed his face as Spud, the therapy dog, happily greeted him. Kyle kneeled down to pet Spud while taking in my office, comfortable chairs, colorful rugs, and bookcases filled with miniatures, games, and artwork.

Spud followed Kyle to the couch as he plopped down and continued to pet his new friend. "Is he your dog?" Kyle asked.

"Yes, Spud is a rescue dog. He was abused when he was younger and then rescued, adopted, and trained as therapy dog." I shared Spud's story and how he would have every reason not to trust humans—but with time and learning to trust, he now helps people.

Kyle didn't look up, but continued to pet him, then said, "That sounds like me."

"Really? In what way?" I asked. Kyle began to open up about being adopted from an orphanage and how he felt unloved. I have never had a resistant child open up so quickly.

I expected it would take many meetings to build trust; it took minutes with Spud in the room. A friendly animal with a meaningful story immediately lowered Kyle's resistance and cultivated a willingness to open up. Spud's story was also a bridge built to believing that if God cared for this mistreated animal, how much more did he care for Kyle and his story?

Expressive therapies distinctively utilize God's creation to provide comfort and resolve struggles, but they must be used with special intentionality to expressly point people to the One who ultimately gives life and meaning. We should actively incorporate these resources because they are instinctively biblical and creational; we need to make sure we use them to the fullest in order to compellingly, proactively point people to the love of their Creator.

As Paul says in Romans 1:20, the universe, creation, and all its creatures are part of the most elegant and lovely story ever revealed, and all point to God. Through creation and the use of general revelation, God communicates his existence, power, and glory to the whole world, so that we are all without excuse. All general revelation is meant to point to its Creator. Does it not make sense, then, that people would find comfort, hope, and perspective when they are exposed to nature? Therefore, we can use what God created to invite people to him!

Every experience with creation teaches a lesson about God's glory. When we step out into creation, there is something about the way we see God that is very experiential and personal. Creation proclaims and bears witness to God's beauty, creative liberty, intelligence, power, authority, tenderness, and majesty.

And we are part of his wonderful creation, a reflection of his wonder and glory. We are fearfully and wonderfully made, Psalm 139:14 reminds us. All of creation is a reminder of God's goodness and provision toward us. It provides a glimpse of the new heavens and earth we will someday enjoy. This is why experiencing creation through expressive therapies can be so key in unlocking the hearts of young people and building a connection with them that will open them up to the healing truths of the gospel.

We are raising kids who are overly scheduled, highly stressed, and more and more lonely and isolated than ever. Because today's children and teens tend to spend more and more time indoors, they are more detached from God's creation than ever before. They spend more time plugged in to screens than swimming or fishing in streams. In his book *Last Child in the Woods: Saving Our Children from Nature-Deficit Disorder*, author Richard Louv researched how young people are being impacted by the deprivation of engaging with creation. His research indicates that those who spend time in nature are healthier, less prone to illness, less stressed, and more adaptable.[7] We can understand this as creation points us to a Creator who reminds us who he is and what our own place is in this world.

If all creation points to a Creator, and counseling is meant to point young people to the One who knows them, and to allow the Spirit to work and move and flourish in their lives, then it is good and right then that we winsomely and wisely apply creation to the process of counseling.

HOW CAN WE USE EXPRESSIVE ACTIVITIES OR CREATION IN COUNSELING?

So, how and when do we employ these activities in our counseling? We all want a formula: do this, don't do this, say this, follow these three steps. But we will miss the person in front of us if we do not seek wisdom from God first. Counseling tools, methods, and resources are helpful and provide insight; however, they can never replace a biblical understanding of human nature and the wisdom to know what to do with it.

Many counselors debate how directive (didactic/instructive) or nondirective (withholding interpretation/evaluation) we are to be when working with a child or adult. Some argue that counselors should be more relational and less didactic, while others push to be more directive and less passive. The picture below presents a balanced approach based on biblical wisdom.

WISDOM IN APPROACH

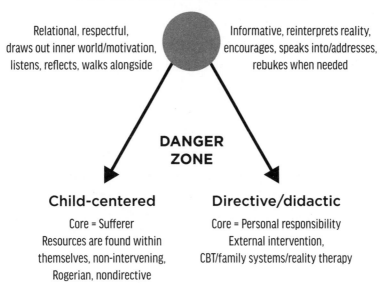

God as Father & Wise Counselor

Relational, respectful, draws out inner world/motivation, listens, reflects, walks alongside

Informative, reinterprets reality, encourages, speaks into/addresses, rebukes when needed

DANGER ZONE

Child-centered

Core = Sufferer
Resources are found within themselves, non-intervening, Rogerian, nondirective

Directive/didactic

Core = Personal responsibility
External intervention,
CBT/family systems/reality therapy

Fundamentally, a biblical worldview will lean toward more directive than nondirective counseling. Why? Because we know from Scripture that we need counsel outside ourselves. Left to our own devices, we are prone to wander and come to faulty conclusions. Inaccurate interpretations, and conclusions lead us away from Christ. Proverbs 3:5–6 reminds us that we need the Lord's leading: "Trust in the Lord with all your heart, and do not lean on your own understanding. In all your ways acknowledge him, and he will make straight your paths."

Young people need us to help them not only make accurate sense out of their lives and experiences, but in doing so lead them to the One who gives meaning. The Genesis account tells us that humans were created dependent on God for perspective and wisdom. As individuals, we do not have enough wisdom and perspective in ourselves.

God, our Father, is the source of all wisdom and also embodies a relational, empathic understanding. This is displayed preeminently in the incarnation of Jesus, who is the expressed image of the Father (Colossians 1:13–23). Hebrews 4:15–16 adds, "we do not have a high priest who is unable to sympathize with our weaknesses, but one who in every respect has been tempted as we are, yet without sin. Let us then with confidence draw near to the throne of grace, that we may receive mercy and find grace in our time of need."

Christ is also directive, and offers a reorienting perspective for us. We see how he displayed the Father's heart in the way he engaged the woman at the well (John 4:1–42). Jesus saw her, noticed her, moved toward her, engaged her, and sought to know her—in order to help her know herself. He is one who draws near to us.

As a result, the woman "left her water jar and went away into town and said to the people, 'Come and see a man who told me all that I ever did. Can this be the Christ?' Then they went out of the town and were coming to him" (vv. 28–30). The people were won over by how Jesus treated the woman and by what Jesus revealed to them. Jesus's willingness to know the woman inspired confidence and trust in him. We all need to be known and we all need wisdom outside of ourselves—wisdom that comes from God.

Nonetheless, while directive counseling is often called for, it is also extremely important to listen, reflect, and allow space and time for an individual to consider what he or she is doing or hearing. Expressive activities can facilitate this process by providing a nonthreatening, relaxing environment. We want to encourage children and young people to process and work through feelings, situations, or life events and to feel fully heard. Without allowing space for a young person to reflect and process out loud, we can miss the real need in front of us because we are focused on what we perceive the child needs.

Let me demonstrate. Years ago a single mother, Liv, brought her very young daughter, Mattie, to me. Liv was concerned that a possible situation of mistreatment occurred in her daughter's school. I put thought into how I could draw this little girl out and try to discern what was going on. I took Mattie over to rows of miniature animals I have in my office and allowed her to pick some out that we could use to role-play. Mattie was attracted to a group of little miniature dogs and grabbed a handful of them. We carefully placed them on the table where we were working, and I began formulating a role-play about the specific topic that concerned her mother. I asked how a little doggie might respond to the circumstance.

Mattie responded by changing the story line and talking about the little puppy that never got to see her father. The puppy was upset that she did not recognize the daddy dog. I responded by acknowledging what she said and then gently directed her back to the role-play I had initiated. I asked another question about how the puppy might respond to the concerns of the mother. Mattie went back to her story and repeated the same scenario she had given me. I acknowledged her story, and then proceeded to redirect her back to my story.

Once again, when it was her turn, she shared how the puppy was afraid that the daddy dog would be angry at her for not visiting. The puppy feared that she would soon forget what the father looked like. The puppy was afraid that the daddy dog was very angry and blamed her for not visiting.

It was then that the light bulb went on. I looked over at her mother, Liv, only to see her shocked by the revelation. I asked Mattie to tell me more, and she proceeded to share how the little puppy had not seen the daddy dog in a very long time and she was beginning to forget what the daddy looked like. She was afraid and upset that the daddy dog would be upset with her for forgetting what he looked like and for not coming to visit.

It became abundantly clear that my agenda was not as important as addressing what was on the mind and heart of this little girl. As I joined her in the story and asked more questions, I saw tears forming in her mother's eyes. I asked the little puppy to ask mommy dog what she thought was going on. Then, with her daughter's permission, I invited Liv into the role-playing scenarios.

Mattie had been struggling deeply with the fact that she missed her birth father and had not seen him in a long time. Her mother had no idea this was going on inside of her and that her daughter blamed herself. The activity unveiled a struggle this little girl had going on that no one else knew about.

Here was an expressive activity/role-play being done with a child in order to work through what we assumed was one problem, but actually was a different one on the forefront of this little child's heart. It was a valuable moment of understanding.

Sometimes we can be so focused on what we perceive to be the goal that we miss a very significant need. It made perfect sense that I would move toward this little girl and attempt to resolve the stated goal of counseling that brought her to me. However, it was equally as important that I heard and saw what was more important in that moment.

Many client-centered counselors would argue that this is a prime example of why one should be less directive. I would argue, however, that what it exemplifies is the need for us to model Jesus in the way we engage with people. We will be both thoughtful and directive, while also listening well, observing, and giving room for people to share their inner world.

There is also room for the fact that, as counselors, we may tend to naturally be more directive or more nondirective in our approach to people. There is a lot of liberty here as long as it is the need of the situation, not our personal preferences, that lead the direction of counseling. Our desire to know and engage each person well is what must inform whether we need to be more or less directive. Love for the person in front of us always bids us to evaluate the needs of the moment and bring hope and truth to them.

I almost missed a very important issue in this little girl's life because I was so focused on what I thought was needed. However, you and I should also be encouraged that when the Spirit of God is at work in us, God can redirect us when we are missing something. It is incredibly encouraging to know that even in our mistakes God can work in a person's life. The Lord can open the blind eyes of everyone involved— including us. It is not perfection we are called to, but to a commitment to really know people well. Let's be careful to listen well, be slow to speak, thoughtful to draw out, and wise to speak truth back in.

WHAT WE ARE AIMING TO DO?

Again, expressive activities are projective activities (revealing of one's inner world) that are used for the purpose of helping kids or teens (and even adults) communicate about themselves, their world, their relationships, and their struggles in ways that feel more easily accessible. We then want to be balanced and winsome in speaking hope and truth back into those experiences.

Young people are a work in progress. Because of time, developmental changes, and new seasons of life, they will always have new things to adapt to. At the same time, we have a faithful God who is writing each of their stories.

Everyone is different, with different characters, circumstances, lessons, blessings, sufferings, twists, and turns. The Lord desires to take the blessings and sufferings of each unruly character and weave them together in an amazing narrative of redemption and love. We want to help children understand their stories, and point them to the Author of those stories. They are still being written, and we want to teach them that the Author of the story is good and that he can be trusted implicitly.

Chapter 5

Principles and Application

Often people assume that if you work with kids, it must come easy to you. I suppose for a select few this might be true, but for the rest of us it is not. Engaging meaningfully with a child or teen takes hard work and can be exhausting. The regular practice of thinking and relating to young people on their level requires commitment and thinking outside of the box, as well as a constant pursuit of insight and wisdom.

Because the work is so difficult, it's tempting to rely on our own capabilities and natural inclinations to love and counsel well. But that can easily lead us to a formulaic approach and cause us to miss the variety of needs in front of us. The wide scope of situations and personalities we encounter in counseling stretches us beyond our natural capacity and reminds us that we need the Spirit of God living and working in us to do that which feels uncomfortable and outside our skill set. The added challenge of engaging with children can tempt us to look for the easiest and quickest solutions to their struggles, rather than doing the hard work of discerning what is most beneficial to the young people we are serving.

It seems simple, maybe even obvious, that we would need to constantly depend on the Lord for wisdom and discernment in counseling. Yet we often find that we are trying to function with no sense of God's personal involvement in the process. We perform within our own skills and abilities, giving very little thought to how Christ would play a part in the moment. We must be confident not in our own ability, but in God's ability to work within us and give us the resources we need to love, understand, and speak truth.

RELY ON GOD'S WORD

When assessing the needs in front of us and seeking to speak life and truth into the challenges at hand, Scripture will be our anchor. God's Word not only teaches us relational wisdom but shows us how the gospel speaks to all heart issues and life situations. It gives us discernment to know how to lovingly engage issues of anger, grief, discipline, parenting, long-suffering, and more.

Scripture gives us the foundational understanding of who we each are in relationship to Christ, what he has done for us, and how our ministry as counselors flows from the desire to connect our counselees to these life-giving truths. This bedrock gives us a heart for discipling well (listening, exercising patience, teaching, guiding, and training), while the Spirit supplies us with the wisdom and commitment needed to apply Scriptural counsel to each individual's life and struggles. If you are interested in growing in a biblical framework for your counseling, The Christian Counseling and Educational Foundation (www.ccef.org) has a wealth of rich resources.

It is essential that we steep ourselves in thinking deeply and biblically about life and our understanding of people. Scripture "has granted to us all things that pertain to life and godliness" (2 Peter 1:3) and it "is breathed out by God and profitable for teaching, for reproof, for correction, and for training in righteousness" (2 Timothy 3:16). Commit yourself to knowing what God has to say about the struggles our young people are facing.

RELY ON GOD'S SPIRIT

You and I are not alone in our counseling. The Spirit of God is at work and intimately involved in our lives and ministry. There will be times we do not know what to do or how to respond to the person in front of us. In the moments when we feel confused, lost, or heartbroken from what we hear, we can trust the Spirit will intercede and direct us, giving us insight into the help that our counselee needs. Romans 8:26 reminds us that even when we do not know what to pray, the Holy Spirit intercedes on our behalf.

It is equally encouraging to know that the Spirit of God directs us. John 16:13 reminds us, "When the Spirit of truth comes, he will guide you into all the truth, for he will not speak on his own authority, but whatever he hears he will speak, and he will declare to you the things that are to come."

We also know from John 14:26 that "the Helper, the Holy Spirit, whom the Father will send in my name, he will teach you all things and bring to your remembrance all that I have said to you." There will be times we feel perplexed or caught off guard, but we are never in it alone. We have a Helper who instructs, comforts, reminds, and intercedes.

QUALITIES COUNSELORS NEED TO WORK WITH YOUNG PEOPLE

When thinking about the type of counselor who is most effective with children, the temptation is to think that a happy, assertive, high-energy, fun, and warm personality is the most important thing to look for. Similarly, if you work with teens, you may think you must be cool, funny, hip, trendy, gregarious, and an extrovert. While these qualities do seem to be advantageous in connecting with young people, they can sometimes be emphasized too much.

Some of the wisest and most effective counselors I know are naturally introverted, laid-back, and meek in nature, but they are incredibly gifted at making people (including teens) feel cared for. Nothing substitutes for genuine care and interest in a young person. Children and teens can be amazingly insightful at spotting counterfeit care and concern. Likewise, whether or not we think we are wired to work with young people, they will sense when someone genuinely listens and is fond of them.

I believe we can grow and develop skills in working with children and teens, even if we don't feel it comes naturally. These skills will grow as you ask the Spirit to give you a deep and genuine love for the children you are counseling.

What does love look like when speaking with children and young people? Below are some specific ways we can show a child that we are genuinely interested in them and committed to loving them the way God loves them.

- Connection on their developmental level
- Willingness to learn about their world, culture, and experiences
- Patience with noncompliance, distraction, or attention-seeking behaviors
- Kindness when met with sarcasm and defiance
- Ability to listen and take time to make sure they feel understood
- Ability to ask open-ended questions and draw out more information when given short answers
- An understanding that they are limited in their ability to change circumstances
- Willingness to work with parents and the family context
- Ability to stay hands-on and engaged
- Readiness to flex with the mood of a child or teen who does not feel like talking
- Flexibility to have multiple options and plans when your first approach does not succeed
- Willingness to be inventive and spontaneous and adapt as needed
- Ability to be light-hearted and engaging
- Perseverance when met with resistance

PRACTICAL WAYS TO SHOW LOVE

When we minister to a young person, we want her to feel we understand her. The skill is to draw out a young person; the gift is to really understand. No amount of skill can substitute for genuine care and "knowing" a child.

Children can throw curveballs at us on a regular basis, so we must be willing to meet them in the moment, engage them with what is important to them, and always have an eye for where we need to direct them.

We must avoid coming across as fake or patronizing. We must not try to pretend to be cool or act like something we are not. It is helpful to be contemporary and "in the know," but young people have a sense for adults who really aren't up to speed with their world and sense the patronizing nature of those who pretend they are more informed than they actually are. It is far better to be a genuine caring adult who is slightly "out of it" but willing to learn than an adult who attempts to act cool and hip yet misses the young person.

We need to dress in a way that is comfortable both to us and the age group we are working with. We want to wear clothing that makes it easy for us to sit on the floor, kneel, work our way in and out of role-playing, throwing a ball, or sitting on the floor with a puzzle, with puppets, or miniatures. We do not want the way we are dressed to limit us from interacting with a youth. We want young people to feel at ease and comfortable—if you and I are dressed in business attire, we can easily feel unrelatable to a child or teen.

PRACTICAL SKILLS IN LOVING CHILDREN THROUGH EXPRESSIVE ACTIVITIES

As we begin to draw children into expressive activities, there are methods that will make an activity fruitful—as well as practices that may set it up to fail. When an interaction with a young person goes off the rails or seems to be an utter failure, it usually has more to do with our skill in approaching a child than it does the activity itself. We are quick to write off an approach as "ineffective" or "unhelpful," when the reality often has more to do with our implementation of the tool.

For example, you may pull out an activity without much preparation, then begin doing it with a child without a clear path of what you hope to accomplish. The directions and examples are unclear, and the child doesn't understand. Therefore, the child gives answers that are not revealing or helpful. You (and perhaps the child) chalk it up as a useless resource. On the other hand, if you had considered why you'd chosen that resource, slowed down, given clear instructions, and paused to discuss it, you likely would have had a very different outcome.

Below are some principles for how to engage well with kids and teens. As you think through this list, keep in mind that there are always exceptions to the norm and that you will want to stay flexible and adapt to the child in front of you.

1. *Give instructions one step at a time.* Give the first step, let them ask questions if they need clarification, then allow them time to complete the task. When given too many steps at one time, children will tend to rush, jump ahead, or forget what we've asked of them. Encourage them to take their time, go slowly, and explain that there is no rush. Your goal is to draw them out, not rush through to completion.

2. *Keep directions simple and clear.* As adults, we can explain too much and often give too many details. You will confuse, lose, bore, and put off young people with the monotony of unnecessary words, lengthy directions, and confusing explanations. Unnecessary words tend to confuse and distract rather than bring clarity. Think through how you will say something. Ask yourself, "Is there a simpler way to say this?" Once you settle on your explanation, do not come up with multiple ways to say it. The more you elaborate, the more you confuse. Children may lose what you are asking them to do because you become too wordy, use complicated language, or present multiple ideas that confuse them.

    For example, if I say, "I want you to write down the people you are closest to, have the best relationship with, or think like you best," I have actually given a child three very different questions. It is better to simply say, "Who are you closest to?" then wait and see what they do with the question. Even if you think you gave unhelpful directions, it might be worth waiting for them to ask for clarity. A child will often say, "What do you mean?" If he or she seems hesitant or confused, you can restate your directions in a new way that he or she may better understand. Even if the child does something very different than what you intended, the response will still be revealing of his or her cognitive ability and situational perception.

3. *Check in with the child to see if he or she understands your instructions.* Simply ask, "Do you have any questions?" Though some children will ask for clarification, some may be afraid to admit they did not understand. You can make sure they are tracking with you by asking them to repeat the instructions back to you.

4. *When asking a child or teen to brainstorm with you, or when they are making a list, avoid asking "Is that it?"* This tends to end the discussion. Rather, asking "What else?" several times throughout the activity will encourage the child that there is more to say. A child or teen will speak longer and share more

when you assume they have more to share, and they will let you know when they really are done.

5. *Consider if it is helpful to complete an activity along with them.* Some kids will like if you model and share your activity as they share theirs. However, children may also be tempted to copy what you do or believe your way must be the right way. I am careful to not complete an activity right alongside them; in my experience, my response can often impact how they shape their own responses.

6. *Consider how and when silence is helpful, or by contrast, uncomfortable.* Many times you can use subtle background music to fill in any uncomfortable silence. Music can soothe, relax, and create a comfortable environment for kids and teens. Some might find it distracting, however, so be prepared to turn it off if necessary. Take cues on how chatty they like to be while they work, or whether they just need to focus. Some children enjoy talking and explaining what they are doing while they work. They may even be more open to sharing hard stuff while their attention is on an activity.

7. *Do not assume you understand a completed project a child presents to you.* Though it may seem obvious, always let them explain their work. Ask them to tell you what they've drawn, what miniature they chose, or what color they used. It is far better to let a child tell you what they have drawn, written, or made than to believe you know what they have done and guess incorrectly. We care about *their* perceptions of what they've created, not ours. When you make your own guesses, you will sometimes misidentify what the child has done—and the child may or may not correct you. This could change the conversation or the child's original thinking on the subject. Some children will correct you if you are wrong, but others will be afraid to.

   Be careful also of wording things in such a way that your assumption is implied. For example, instead of asking a child "Why did you pick that purple frog?" a more helpful response would be, "Tell me what you picked to represent your mom. Why did you pick that?"

8. *Ask open-ended questions whenever possible.* "Yes" and "no" questions tend to end a conversation, while open-ended questions—questions that can't be answered with a simple "yes or "no"—foster explanation. It is also better to ask "what" questions rather than "why" questions. "Why" questions can be helpful to ask when you want to understand the reason a child chose a particular object or gave a particular answer, but it is also easy for a child to shrug and say, "I don't know." "What" questions such as "What was going on in the picture?" tend to promote better discussion.

When we come to the expressive activities I outline later in the book, you'll see that I often ask kids to brainstorm with me. They could be brainstorming all the potential possibilities for what they are thinking, feeling, why they are feeling it, etc. Young people often don't know what they are thinking or why they did what they did. Perhaps they had multiple, conflicting reasons for why they are upset, or how they would answer a question. They often feel the pressure of one correct answer. Perhaps they feel pressure to answer difficult questions on the spot but aren't prepared to. When this happens, children tend to shut down, say "I don't know," or shrug and give the answer they believe you are looking for. When I say, "Let's brainstorm all the possible things that make you anxious," I allow them to have more than one answer or one reason. It feels less threatening for a child to know that there could be many reasons or options to consider. I have found that when we allow kids and teens to brainstorm or provide a list of ideas, they often reveal what is going on. If you asked a child "Why were you anxious?" you may get an answer, even a somewhat accurate one, but it might not be a complete answer. If you say instead, "Let's brainstorm on this paper all the things that make you anxious," you will likely get a fuller picture of all the things going on inside the child.

9. *Be relaxed and conversational.* You want kids to feel they are in a safe place where they are free to be vulnerable, open up about their situation, make mistakes, and express thoughts and ideas.

10. *Have a Plan A, a Plan B, and a Plan C!* When you are getting to know a child, you are learning what works and what doesn't. You are choosing tools and methods to get to know them and draw them out. An activity may or may not work for multiple reasons: a child or teen doesn't connect with what you are doing; you haven't explained the activity clearly; the child is simply in a bad mood, tired, hungry, cranky, or distracted. You may be able to come back to the activity at a later time and have it well received; but also be prepared that, for whatever reason, you may need to abandon ship and try a different approach. When you have multiple options that will serve your goal, you can be flexible as you interact. If an activity seems to be going very poorly, you have the freedom to toss it aside and try a new approach. There are many ways to speak into and draw out a child's world, and as a counselor you are looking for an open door. If one door seems closed or locked, go around and try a new one.

11. *Offer to be the "secretary."* When a young person is sharing thoughts or ideas, volunteer to write down the details. When applicable, I like to write their words directly on the activity to emphasize that what they say is important.

Most children do not like to write; it feels like homework, is laborious, and slows down their thinking and expression. When you say, "Your ideas are important. I want to remember what you said, so I will be your secretary," they feel cared for and understood. It also helps you to remember what they said word-for-word, rather than to rely on your perception of what they communicated.

Remember, even when an activity seems to fail, you have likely learned something important about the child you are counseling. It will reveal something about the child—their developmental level, their cognitive ability, or where they are emotionally, spiritually, or socially. How self-aware or unaware are they? Does he think in abstractions, does he rush, or does he have limited attention? Does he enjoy drawing or journaling, or hate it? Everything you learn helps you piece together the puzzle before you.

Chapter 6

Methods for Drawing Out Children and Teens

I love Proverbs 20:5, which I have already quoted repeatedly in this book. It aptly reminds us that we are called to be wise people, committed to drawing out the inner motives of the heart. Much of our success or failure at drawing out children has more to do with the winsome skillfulness of an adult than it does the ability of young people to articulate themselves. Most young people struggle to know their own motives; as adults, we need to bring the persevering care and capability to help them, always careful that we are quick to listen and slow to speak (James 1:19), making every effort to know and understand a child so that we can sagely speak into their experience.

Below, you will find examples of methods that are helpful in working with young people.

Especially in these next couple chapters, I have attempted to include resources, methods, ideas, and activities that can be adapted for almost any age. In every case, you will need to consider why you are using them and how you'd adapt them to your situation. We often assume teenagers will find something juvenile or silly about an activity and dismiss it before giving it a chance. We might also expect very young children to make connections or see cause and effect in unhelpful places. There will always be reasons that something may or may not work for the child you are working with. Therefore, always remember:

- You are adapting your activity to the child in front of you. Consider what you are hoping to learn about them.
- Most expressive activities can be modified to fit elementary kids or teenagers.
- Take your time doing the activity. It is not an item to check off your list; there is no set time frame. Your goal is to build bridges of trust and relationship and open doors to better know your child.

- It is good to stop and talk about things that come out while doing the activity. Don't simply focus on an end result (completing the task) but really invest in the process (learning, knowing, and seeing the world through their eyes).
- Be creative. Always feel free to adapt, change, or build on any activity to make it better or more useful for your situation.

STRATEGIC USE OF BOOKS AND STORYTELLING

Great stories teach us about life, love, self-sacrifice, forgiveness, and the dangers of pride and corruption. Each contains a lesson to instruct and equip with important truths. As such, storytelling has long been a tradition of education and has served as a key method of passing down traditions and cultural beliefs, instilling moral values, and reminding a new generation of its history.

From oral tradition to the use of fables and parables to the invention of the written word, stories have long moved people, educated cultures, and driven home a message (good or bad). Short stories or fables (the latter often with animals or inanimate objects as characters) can be constructively used to teach a moral lesson. Through the use of good literature—including books, stories, poems, fairy tales, fables, and letters—truths are reiterated in a disarming way and capture a young person's attention.

We tell stories and read books to children to educate them and to build communication skills that connect us relationally. In today's culture, storytelling and reading is a decreasing family practice, because it requires extra time and a slowing down of a typical day's routine. Keeping the habit of storytelling alive, however, can enhance bonds within families as well as instill essential beliefs in a child's heart and mind.

From a developmental standpoint, children are constantly learning about emotions—theirs and others'. Good books can help them learn to recognize what emotions they are feeling, what emotions others have, how such emotions impact everyone, and what to do and how to respond in healthy, godly ways. Books can teach important skills that will help children learn appropriate behaviors for emotions, begin to understand cause and effect, and learn responsibility in relationships. If a child is on the autism spectrum and has difficulty engaging socially, books can be a helpful way to model how to navigate various relational scenarios.

Good stories help encourage healthy social behavior, clarify values, and instill cultural identity. They teach discernment in relationships, and provide opportunities for modeling and improving communication.

Culture is telling its own story, communicating a narrative of what is true, morally good, and socially acceptable. This story is pervasive in movies, social media, magazines, and children's education. The cultural narrative of today indoctrinates children with an increasingly godless worldview. Right is often treated as wrong, and wrong is often treated as being right. Children need help making sense of what they are hearing, which also means they need proactive instruction about what is true and right and good.

Children benefit from seeing their own struggles worked out through the use of story. Acting bravely, overcoming a bully, or learning to resolve conflict resonate more deeply when we see it played out before us. Some young people love writing their own stories and can work through personal struggles by projecting their thoughts and feelings onto a character in a story.

When reading or telling a story, make sure to explicitly connect the dots back to a child's life and experiences. What might be obvious to us needs to be made clear for a child or teen. For example, when I am trying to help young children identify feelings, I often use a book by Dr. Seuss called *My Many Colored Days*. The story illustrates how colors can also express feelings and moods; it leads into an expressive activity I then work on with the child.

With children who have more abstract thinking and maturity, I look for books that relate to their lives and struggles, and then find ways to weave that into the counseling process. Some young people hate reading but enjoy being read to; others relate better to watching the story unfold on a screen. For teens, stories may be best told in person through movies, poems, songs, or a YouTube video or testimony. Whatever form you use, be thoughtful in connecting the dots for them in ways that produce change, growth, and hope, and which point them to truth.

There is no greater story than the one given to us in Scripture. A great deal of Scripture is in narrative story form. There is a unified biblical narrative of creation, fall, redemption, and restoration. It is our story and must be *the story* that shapes the lives and hearts of our young people, providing a lens for all other stories they will hear. In counseling, we can and must become better at telling this amazing story in ways that capture the affections of children and teens. The better we become at bringing Scripture to life for kids, the more likely they are to embrace its truths for themselves. We need to help them map onto the story of the Scripture in ways that transform their lives and their experiences. We want to give our young people hope that everything they go through will be redeemed and used by God. He makes all things new.

Many times, children and teens feel disconnected from the Lord and the Bible. Talking about Scripture as a story helps young people to connect with the Lord and his unchangeable character. In his story, God is portraying his glory and character, restoring all things, and leading his children back to himself. It is vital that when we work with young people, we look for ways to weave in biblical truth, and then connect their life, experiences, and needs back to the Lord.

There are a wide variety of literary styles used in the Bible, including narrative, poetry, sermons, and letters. Instruction is provided both directly and indirectly. In counseling we can access each of these scriptural forms to connect with the young person in front of us. A look through the Psalms will show a teen that they can be honest with God about their deep emotions. A parable of Jesus will break down a theological concept in a way a child can understand. A look at the cross will describe the deep sacrificial love of the Lord.

Further examples will be given in the next chapter, but the possibilities are endless as we become more winsome and wise in connecting young people to Scripture. Consider how to become better at using both ordinary stories and more importantly, Scripture, to encourage real change in the lives of children and teens.

Superheroes and villains in counseling

Superheroes

Superheroes have fostered tremendous inspiration and imagination in the lives of young people. There are many reasons that children and teens are drawn into a superhero story or movie. Superheroes possess larger-than-life capabilities, triumphantly rise above conflict and misfortune, give a sense of hope in the presence of tragedy, show courage in the face of oppression, and demonstrate good conquering evil. They provide examples of victors overcoming adversity and underdogs achieving the impossible. Because of this, superheroes can readily be used to connect with children in counseling.

Children become quickly attached to exciting rescue stories. These narratives can provide an avenue for children and teens to use their imagination to bring their own stories and uniqueness to life.

There are many additional winning characteristics that draw us to superheroes. They are intriguing and engaging. They are enough like us to make them relatable, but different enough to make us wish we could do the things they do. They are complex and mysterious, leaving us wondering what makes them tick. We find they often rise out of tragedy or hardship and then move forward with a mission and a purpose greater than themselves. They use their new identity to fight crime, bigotry, evil, and racism. They possess qualities to be admired by all: selflessness, loyalty, patriotism, and compassion, to name a few.

What kids can sometime miss is the ways superheroes are encumbered by both their secret identity and their moral obligation to use their powers to combat evil. Often a superhero feels like an outsider and lives a lonely life. He or she is misunderstood by those around him or her and remains in disguise, never really feeling known by others.

In these ways, young people can also relate.

Superheroes can be used by counselors and other adults to build bridges with young people. Kids will enjoy bringing you into their interests, hobbies, and even their superhero obsession. It is also a great segue into a young person's own experiences. You can ask thoughtful questions like:

- Tell me what you enjoy about the story of Star Wars.
- Who is your favorite character? Why?
- Do you relate with his/her struggles?
- How have you felt that way in life?

In addition to this, with great power comes great responsibility, and the weight of such accountability burdens superheroes. They carry the burden of knowing that everyone they get close to is at risk of harm from the villains they battle. In addition, each superhero has an Achilles' heel—something that threatens to expose him or her and lead to his or her destruction.

The themes or emotions associated with loneliness, burdens of responsibility, and hidden weaknesses are themes we also see in the lives of the children we counsel. Connecting them to a story of another can often help them see how their hardship can be used for good. More importantly, they can open the door to help children dream bigger dreams of a God who is more powerful than any superhero they can create in their imaginations—someone who is real, personal, and truly does fight battles on their behalf.

Sometimes when we use superhero stories to enter into the world of the imaginary with children, we free them to express their inner world without limits. Associating with stories outside of themselves helps reveal a picture of their deepest wishes, thoughts, motives when given the ability to express it through play and diversion.

Spider-Man is the story of young Peter Parker, who is driven by guilt and remorse. Peter comes home to find that a criminal he had ignored for selfish reasons killed his uncle Ben. He is scarred by the sin he committed and driven by anguish to right his wrongs. He battles feelings of guilt and his inability to keep his family safe. He is a picture of a superhero who is a victim himself, battling his own demons. Superheroes in this category feel misunderstood, alone, and isolated. How might this type of story map onto the experience of a child who has been through a tragedy and is battling a mix of grief and regret?

If a young person gravitates toward Spider-Man, ask questions like:

- What do you like about the Spider-Man story/movies?
- Are there ways you connect to his struggle? How?
- Do you ever feel misunderstood? Alone?

- What are the demons you battle?
- Do you ever feel you have to redeem yourself? How?

There is also the story of the Incredible Hulk. He is plagued, even tortured, by his uncontrollable rage, his struggles coming as a result of abuse he suffered at the hands of his father. There are strong themes to explore here, particularly how being victimized can impact a child both emotionally and psychologically. Even children who have not been the victims of abuse often struggle with controlling their anger and can readily relate to how the Hulk behaves.

A child who has been mistreated or struggles with anger may gravitate toward the story of the Hulk. You can also use the story, sympathizing with the Hulk's struggle with anger and mistreatment. Consider discussing:

- Why do you think the Hulk gets so angry?
- Have you ever felt that way? When?
- What does the Hulk do with his anger?
- How does that make him feel more isolated and alone?
- What do you do with your anger?
- Does it help or tend to make things worse for you?
- Where can we go for real help with our anger?

Can you see how taking story lines from characters that kids and teens relate to can also connect dots to their lives—and then connect dots to the person of Christ, who really does equip them with supernatural resources for life?

Superman, perhaps one of the most iconic superheroes, is an alien, an outsider from another planet. He lost his birth family at a young age, was orphaned, and then adopted. Can you imagine the number of children who can identify with his story? Consider asking these questions:

- What powers do you wish you had?
- What do you think it was like to be Superman?
- What do you think his life was like?
- In what ways is Superman imperfect?
- Do you think he ever felt alone? Misunderstood?

For more ideas on how to approach this, refer to the "If I Were a Superhero" worksheet in the next chapter.

Villains

Sometimes as you get to know a child, he will readily share his love of particular stories, movies, and characters. Many young people love adventure or fantasy stories with strong themes of good and evil, a battle to save the world, and clearly defined heroes and villains. Popular examples that often emerge are the Star Wars or Lord of the Rings series. Most often children and youth are drawn to these narratives for the noble role the hero plays in defeating a formidable, unassailable foe against all odds.

What do you do, however, with kids who may feel more drawn to the villain in a story? An affinity for the "bad guy" may grow for many reasons. Children can feel misunderstood in the way a villain does in a story. They see that the villain was bullied or mistreated early on and feel empathy toward him or her. A child may identify with the desire to get even with those who have wronged her, and may even like the power that the villain wields as he or she strikes out against his or her enemies.

Many villains demonstrate tremendous creative genius and ingenuity. The problem is that they use such skills for selfish or sinister gain. They are usually bent on destroying the hero and grow an insatiable desire for power and control. Villains are self-absorbed, narcissistic, and fail to learn from their own downfalls. They ultimately self-destruct and become their own demise.

When the children we counsel are drawn to such characters, we want to understand what's behind the attraction to the antihero. This affinity will often reveal deeper struggles—perhaps being misjudged or misperceived, unaccepted, or victimized themselves.

In many cases kids are drawn to villains for the same reason many of us are drawn to the hero—they identify with the character's experience, desires, or struggles. We want to learn how to make a connection between these real experiences and battles our counselees face, and then help guide their attention toward a redemptive narrative that will acknowledge the seriousness of a child's struggles but also direct them to the ultimate righter of wrongs.

We are all prone to wander. We are all prone to use even our strengths for our own selfish desires. Both superheroes and villains have decisions to make. Will they turn to their own devices and be corrupted by their desires, or will they live selflessly for something greater than themselves? We want to call young people to live for the glory of God—*Someone* who is greater and worthy of their allegiance.

Consider the insights we could gain by asking, What would you do if you could . . .

- fly and move at super speed?
- travel through time?
- change shape?
- be invisible?
- have superhuman strength?
- commit crimes without detection?

- see the future?
- have the ability to inflict revenge?
- control another person?

As these conversations develop, we must consider how to utilize our counseling sessions to foster a change of mindset in children. Children desire to exist in a world where they feel in total control of their circumstances. How can we teach them to rest in a real, loving God who is fully in charge of the outcome? Children do not need to take matters into their own hands, nor give in to the temptation to seek their own justice. There is One who fights their battles and overcomes all evil in the end.

Consider the passage in Exodus 14 when God is about to deliver the Israelites from the Egyptians by parting the Red Sea. Moses assures the people, "Fear not, stand firm, and see the salvation of the Lord, which he will work for you today. For the Egyptians whom you see today, you shall never see again. **The Lord will fight for you**, and you have only to be silent" (Exodus 14:13–14, emphasis added).

Earlier I said that many of our struggles with engaging young people are not simply due to their inability to articulate themselves, or their immaturity or short-sightedness; more often, it is due to our inability to draw them out and woo them to what is true and real. Imagine if we took everything that is supernatural, magical, and attractive about the realm of fantasy superheroes and painted a better, more vivid, more captivating portrait of God and his ways. We must do a better job of displaying God's power, authority, miraculous intervention, and very personal care.

Even the greatest, most powerful superhero has weaknesses, downfalls, and struggles with loss and isolation. These figures are limited, flawed, and only a fantasy. When we help kids understand that the greatest value in superheroes is that they point us to the ultimate Victor, we guide them closer to a living God who is in every way the best hero—stronger, better, more dynamic, more loving, more powerful, and more personally involved in their lives than anyone else could ever be.

STRATEGIC USE OF ROLE-PLAYING

Another approach I often use with my children and in counseling is role-playing. Role-playing is the practice of presenting a situation to a child and asking him or her what they would do or say in that situation or story. For example, a child may not know what to do when being taunted aggressively by another child, or when a peer pressures her to lie, cheat, or do or say something harmful to another child. Role-playing gives children an avenue to practice possible responses to difficult situations. This practice can also provide children with the necessary words and actions to use in difficult or uncomfortable situations.

As counselors, role-playing helps us understand how a child thinks and provides us the opportunity to speak back into the child's life. Hearing their responses to scenarios gives us a window into their fears, their temptations, and where they might be caught off guard or unprepared. Children think in black-and-white terms. As a result, it can be challenging for them to wisely navigate the gray areas in life.

In counseling, I talk a great deal about safety skills and evaluating behavior. I will often say, "If someone tells you the right thing to do, you should always listen, regardless of who it is: an adult, stranger, babysitter, friend, or sibling. Conversely, if anyone ever tells you the wrong thing to do, whether a friend, sibling, adult, stranger or babysitter, you should never do it, and we will support you." I will then go on to talk about some examples of wrong things an adult, babysitter, or peer might ask them to do. This might be silly things, like playing risky practical jokes, to reckless things like running down the middle of the road, to completely inappropriate things such as undressing or taking nude photos.

Inevitably, a child will ask, "What if I don't know if what they are asking me is bad?" I will encourage them to brainstorm some examples of confusing scenarios and we will talk through what they might say or do. A grey area might be that an adult they know approaches and asks a child to help them carry something to a private, isolated location, or be asked to get in a car to run to the store. These things don't look "wrong" but may strike a child as uncomfortable, or make them uncertain. In those cases, I always encourage them to go find another adult and get their input.

When helping children who have been victimized, it is important to start teaching them ways they can respond should anyone make them feel uncomfortable or unsafe. Helping them grow means also giving them the skills to know what to do in confusing situations like the ones mentioned above. Role-playing these situations is a great way to create possible scenarios a child may find himself in and practice how he would respond. It is teaching the skill of evaluating a situation and then giving him multiple ways he could act in response.

Role-playing allows children to think *with you* about situations they haven't yet encountered. As you use this tool you'll want to provide a spectrum of possibilities, from the silly, to the obvious, to the confusing, to the dangerous, to that which would never seem possible. Brainstorming a spectrum of scenarios will help engage conversation. When you have a teachable moment, you can take principles that apply in one situation (demonstrating love, kindness, mercy, forgiveness, or safety skills) and transfer them into different situations. This primes children to take one principle and apply it to a multitude of contexts they might not have considered and prepares them for the many situations that may or may not happen.

For example, you could develop a situation where a child is tempted to be an aggressor (maybe with a younger sibling) and speak about reacting to annoyances with love and patience. You could then follow that sketch with a scenario in which the child is a victim in some way, and walk through how to get out of that unhealthy situation.

I have found that the more I am willing to talk about the many "what ifs" with children, the more they are willing to say, "I don't know. What do I do when that happens?" Role-playing opens the door for conversation and for direct input into a child's struggles. By asking kids questions that encourage them to think and make decisions, we help them avoid being stuck in many situations where they don't know what to do.

As children mature and learn to navigate sticky or uncomfortable situations, don't forget to find every opportunity to encourage them. They won't always get it right, but neither do we. It's important to tell children, "Do your best and we will be proud of you. And if you do get it wrong, we will talk about what happened." This assures children that they won't be blamed for mistakes when trying to apply what they've learned from us. Remind them that it's important to discuss all of the trial and error so that we can celebrate what went right and help them consider different ways to respond if an attempt doesn't go well.

Puppets

Puppets can provide another outlet for children to express their inner world. Expressive involvement by the use of puppets can be projective, fun, engaging, and help children lower their guard to interact more honestly with what they are thinking and feeling.

Turning toys into animate objects helps children externalize inner conflicts, beliefs, values, and desires. They also help children display the presence or lack of relational skills. Through the use of play, pretend, and role-playing, children can risk saying things to a puppet about what they really think or feel that they could or would not say directly to a person for fear of negative reaction. Using these objects as tools provides a window of understanding into how children really think, feel, and perceive the world:

- They help expand the expression of inner thoughts and ideas.
- They enhance self-disclosure as well as self-awareness.
- They can help a child better understand good and evil, or right versus wrong.
- They help them vocalize thoughts or questions they may feel unsafe asking for themselves.
- They help show confusion a child may have over life events, or inaccurate views they have embraced.

Children will sometimes act out onto a puppet some kind of harm that has been done to them. Some will act out how they wish they could respond to those around them. A child may superimpose thoughts or emotions onto a puppet that they perceive unacceptable to admit for themselves. A child who is abused may never self-disclose, but might acknowledge to a police-officer puppet that he or she was mistreated by a dragon. A child with extreme anger toward a parent may willingly project it onto a puppet of a dog, while never feeling the freedom to admit it for themselves. Other children will act out relational conflict between two puppets in ways that will help us begin to offer resources or solutions. In helping children engage with puppets and finding new ways to role-play, we can help them transfer those same principles and skills into their real lives.

Katie is a reserved eleven-year-old girl who feels tremendous anxiety about taking the bus to school and moderate anxiety about school in general. She has had meltdowns about leaving the house in the morning, often missing the bus and having a parent drive her to school, only to have another meltdown in the school parking lot before entering.

When Katie began counseling, she was hard to draw out—she answered many questions with "I don't know" or a shrug and would withdraw when hard topics were brought up. She did, however, start to gravitate toward the puppets, and one in particular: the turtle puppet.

I asked if she ever felt like the turtle. She said she did. I asked what she thought the turtle felt inside. She began telling me that the turtle hated mean people and felt that the only way to avoid them was to be invisible. As she was describing the turtle's reaction, she put her hand in the puppet and made it retreat into its shell.

I asked if I could talk to the turtle; she nodded his head. So the turtle and I began talking about the things that made him feel safe and unsafe. I asked him to tell me what helped him feel safe around someone, and the turtle began to answer me. Through the course of a couple of sessions, Katie eventually began talking without the turtle.

Another puppet I've found particularly helpful in counseling is that of a caterpillar that transforms into a butterfly. There are so many productive ways to use a puppet like this to either draw out a child or speak back into his or her life. One helpful way is simply to let it demonstrate how counseling can help the child you're talking to. Just as the caterpillar goes through many changes in the metamorphosis process, so do we as we work through life's struggles and difficulties.

You can also use it as a metaphor for how God works in our lives. A caterpillar's life goes through tremendous change from life as a caterpillar to new life as a butterfly. We can use this reality to illustrate that sometimes we do not understand why something is happening to us, or why we feel we are stuck in the midst of hard things in our life, even though God is up to something good. He wants to do a beautiful work in us. Counseling, getting help, and letting others in can all be part of the process of turning something hard into something really good. A tool like this puppet can help a child begin to grasp that when difficult or confusing things happen to him or her, God can do some of his most magnificent work.

There are so many different puppets that are great for creating metaphors, telling stories, and fostering conversation. Adding these tools to our collection will prove to be valuable in our work with children.

Sand trays

Simply put, sand trays are various type of containers filled with sand that can be used to help people of all ages work through problems in a risk-free environment. A variety of miniatures are also often used. Figures of people of various ethnicities, ages, and disabilities; animals (both aggressive and friendly); bugs; buildings; fences; trees and shrubs; religious symbols; transportation; fantasy figures; and many other miscellaneous objects can be used to take on meaning and roles for kids.

As young people are required to open up emotionally during counseling, sharing their deepest thoughts and feelings, sand trays can provide a protected space and the opportunity to communicate nonverbally. Playing in a structured container, counselees can build a world, real or imaginary, through symbols, miniatures, or other figures; this offers an effective way for individuals to express themselves without words. Children and teens can intuitively pick an object that represents a person, emotion, struggle, idea or dream, hope or fear. This facilitates their ability to share their experiences and feelings in a nonthreatening way.

Children in counseling are able to express in sand things they would otherwise not be able to vocalize or address in traditional therapy. We observe and later analyze the child's interaction with the objects, this small-scale version of their inner world. The world within the sand tray (including the placement and interaction between the miniature toys, figurines, and other objects in the sand) is expressed through symbolism and metaphor, and can help us as counselors to begin recognizing the relationship between the creation in the sand and the child's or teen's inner world.

A small animal or figurine may represent the complexity of something that is both good and bad. For example, I once had a boy pick a set of jelly vampire teeth to represent his mom. When asked why he said, "Because it is soft and she is sweet and kind, but she is also sharp and biting toward me." A teen once picked a pine tree to represent God. When I asked him to share about his choice he said, "Well, it is big, and majestic like I know God is supposed to be, but it does not feel very personal to me." What profound insight we gain when we offer another way for young people to express the complexities they often feel but struggle to articulate.

Sand trays can also be a tool to help those who are "stuck," as they continue to take form and help counselees work through problems. Young people often reenact painful events in a sand tray, attempting to resolve problems or come to a different resolution. Consider the teenager who struggles with school anxiety, who forms a tray to unfold the story of what it's like to go to school. Or perhaps it is the child surviving a high-conflict divorce between his parents, a car accident, a friend's drowning in the lake, or abuse suffered. In these moments, we get to see children externalize what is going on inside, what their perception and interpretation of events are, and we can begin to engage with them.

As a counselor there are times to simply watch and observe, and there are times to enter in, ask questions, and offer solutions or alternative interpretations. We look for ways our counselees are thriving and ways they are distressed. We look for ways to encourage, instruct, correct, and offer hope and healing. We look for ways to retell their story with the Lord as an active player in the middle of it.

One child who had experienced abuse used a sand tray to capture the complexity of all the ways this abuse was impacting her world and the people in her world, from her parents, to her aunts and uncles, to herself.

This child experienced abuse from her father. When it was disclosed, it felt like a tornado had destroyed her family. There is a miniature of a man and woman holding hands running away from a plastic tornado. This represented her father and her aunt who supported him. Her mother is a scared figure lying on the ground, devastated by the news and unable to cope. There are superhero figures and a golden dragon, representing social workers and detectives who entered into the picture. The child talked about them in ways that displayed her fear of them, but also an awareness that they were there to help. A figurine of her home was in the corner, and a fence enclosed the chaotic event.

There was also an opening where a treasure chest sat. The opening represented a way out of the chaos, but also the possibility of entering back in. The treasure chest symbolized the disclosure of abuse, but was closed because "there was still more" to tell. There was more abuse yet to be disclosed, but she was afraid it would cause more harm.

In the far left corner was a little person, which she explained was her. She placed herself as far from the chaos and the tornado as possible. Papa Smurf and Smurfette (her mother's sister and husband) were safe people to stay with; they were like "precious jewels" (plastic jewels placed in the sand) to her. Smurfette (her aunt) stood near the crucifix, because "she always points me to Jesus and takes me to church."

This girl was able to tell of her painful experience by talking about the miniatures, rather than herself, and by projecting the events onto the figures. She shared how both her parents responded, how she felt she was the cause of it all, and how she was processing not only her feelings but the reactions of everyone involved. She could speak of the moments of chaos, and places of reprieve. She could share the uncovering of details and facts—and those still hidden in a treasure chest, too afraid of coming out. She was able to begin to safely tell her story, as well as find help and support as we continued to work on her story through the miniatures.

A sand tray can be static—a single snapshot of their world or an experience. It can also be dynamic—evolving, moving, changing, and progressing as the discussion moves forward. You might ask a child to make a sand tray of everyone in his or her family. This is static—a picture of how the child sees individuals in the home. We might then ask the child to tell a story of being bullied, where the child sets up a sand tray with moving pieces and has the figures interact with one another (a dynamic example). Either method can serve as a helpful tool to draw out a child and give him or her a nonthreatening way to express what is going on inside.

Although the sky's the limit, below is a sampling of topics that can be covered through the use of a sand tray:

- The child's view of his or her world
- Self-image
- A picture of the child's family
- An example of the type of situations that get him or her in trouble
- A demonstration of how he or she gets what he or she wants
- An illustration of how the child feels out of control
- An example of something a child wishes would happen
- Illustrations of things the child is afraid of
- A picture of important relationships
- A demonstration of family rules
- An example of how the child shows love, how the family shows love, etc.
- An illustration of what school, friendships, or even a traumatic event was like
- An example of how the child sees God, or how God interacts with him or her

If you are interested in using miniatures as a resource in counseling, there are many creative ways to make use of them with or without a sand tray. You can use any container or box, or simply a large poster-sized paper to build a picture of their world. I've also built timelines or "maps" and allowed kids to place miniatures on them to represent events or people. The skill is not in the tool itself; it is in how we choose to use it to help people.

STRATEGIC USE OF ART ACTIVITIES

Art and other creative expression can often provide a venue for communication when words don't feel sufficient. This is a wide-open venue for sharing and describing struggles, insights, complex emotions and decisions, perceptions, and relationships.

Various art forms—painting, drawing, coloring, etc.—offer a fresh way to convey beliefs, concerns, and hopes (spoken and unspoken). It can aid in expressing self, understanding personal and relational interactions, and setting goals. Art connects with people of all ages, across the spectrum of abilities, and provides another way to engage the brains, emotions, and hearts of our counselees. You will often see art being used in nursing homes, children's hospitals, and drug and alcohol facilities. There is a way in which art acts as a catalyst to improve brain function, foster self-esteem and self-awareness, enhance social skills, and help reduce and resolve conflicts and distress. Art engages the mind, body, and spirit in ways that are distinct from verbal communication alone, and facilitates open and expressive interaction, which can bypass the limitations of verbal communication.

Art can also be helpful when working with groups. Consider a group of teenage girls who experienced child abuse at a young age. Asking them to create images that represent their hard experiences can serve as a less threatening way for the girls to articulate and reflect on their painful experiences.

Art activities are a great way to build bridges of communication not only between us and our counselees, but also between them and their family members. Many activities can be done together with the family. When parents watch and participate, they can hear and understand their children's experiences in new ways. Kids can also see how their parents feel, think and experience things. In many ways, it levels the playing field between adults and children; they are all doing the same activity and interacting equally on any given topic. This type of exercise can build empathy and compassion for another family member, facilitate better communication, and even nurture a sense of family values or rules.

For those who feel limited in their verbal expression, we demonstrate loving-kindness when we offer another way for them to express their inner world. As Proverbs 20:5 states, we want to be people of understanding and draw out what is going on in the heart. Individuals can often convey more about their emotions and experiences when prompted by images, symbols, and pictures that represent their internal world.

Some sample activities are provided at the end of this chapter. Most of them are open-ended, meaning we have lots of options when using art to see what kids and teens are interested in and how they are able to communicate. I also offer suggestions for how you can hone these activities toward maximum insight and growth for the counselee. As mentioned previously, always feel free to adapt what you are doing to fit the needs of the person in front of you.

Consider asking the young person if he or she likes to talk while creating art, if he or she prefers silence, or if he or she would enjoy music in the background (this can set a relaxing atmosphere). Adapt the environment in a way that facilitates the most engagement with the young person.

Give him or her sufficient time to work on the creative project. Watch quietly or talk with them if they want to dialogue. Sometimes it is helpful to work (or act like we are working) on something quietly right next to them, so they know we are available but do not feel as if they are under the microscope.

It can be tempting to project our own interpretation onto the art project a young counselee creates, and there will be times we have insight or suspicion as to what might be going on in the picture. Remember, however, that it is more important to hear the child's perceptions and ideas than to read it through our own understanding. The goal is to draw out a child's inner world; therefore, listen to how he or she makes sense of it.

STRATEGIC USE OF TECHNOLOGY

To tap into children's imaginations and gain deeper understanding of their problems, counselors are often reaching beyond the customary tools. Some counselors use tablets and smartphones for counseling-related activities, including applications that incorporate art and drawing of pictures, storytelling, and journaling. Asking a child or teen to share pictures of family, friends, pets, and their interests is another way to use technology to connect personally, ask questions, and gather more understanding.

Technology has revolutionized the way many counselors work with children and teens, thus making help more easily accessible. The strategic use of computers, tablets, smartphones, MP3 players, and more can be especially important for counselors who work in settings where the counseling process is often limited by the constraints of space, time, resources, or other responsibilities.

Technology has become such an integral part of much of modern life that there are many strong opinions as to how much it should be incorporated into counseling work with children and teens. Some argue that young people are consumed with screens and media in ways that are both addictive and destructive; therefore, incorporating technology as a tool for counseling further exacerbates the problem. Others argue that children are losing the ability to work with their hands or to sit and engage in conversation and cannot communicate well, and that the use of technology will also prevent this from happening in counseling. Because of these legitimate concerns, care should be given as to why and how we choose to use technology with any child or teen.

When used properly, technology can facilitate opening up children and ministering to them in a way they are comfortable with. One can contend that in order to really build bridges with young people, it is imperative to enter into the world of technology. It is the realm in which many youth are involved: social media, computers/tablets, smartphones, apps, music, etc. Entering into those worlds will give us valuable insights and yield relational capital with children.

And, when carefully used, it can speak back into their struggles. Technology-based programs such as the iPad Playroom: A Therapeutic Technique by Marilyn Snow (which creates a virtual playroom to interact in), Marvel's Superhero Avatar Creator (where you can build your own superhero), and other creative programs have opened the possibility of reaching kids in new ways.

That said, technology is in constant flux. Apps are created and disappear on a regular basis. Therefore, it is important that you do the work of researching what resources might fit your context. I am always careful in how I bring technology into the counseling room. I never want it to replace the importance of building trust and relationship. But when rightly used, it is a tool that connects us to young people and helps maintain connection. It also can provide opportunities to speak back into their lives in ways that are creative and thoughtful.

Even simply discussing pop culture or current media will build rapport in counseling. Many teens will begin to open up when we ask them to share a favorite song or video. We can offer to watch it online with them and discuss what they like about it. Most songs will show the lyrics, which will help us talk about the message and why it appeals to them.

Let's look for ways like this we can open doors into their world. Often when we show interest in what children enjoy, they lower their defenses and willingly allow us to walk right in to speak into their lives.

SAMPLE ART ACTIVITIES

Picture of a Tree

What You Need:

> 12 x 18 paper or larger
> Various art mediums—crayons, colored pencils, markers, etc.

Goals:

Young people will often share more about themselves when asked to draw or imagine themselves in a different form. This exercise attempts to help them think how they see themselves; how others see them; what their perception of strengths, weaknesses, relationships are like—or perhaps how alone or rooted in community they are.

Where a tree is planted (like by streams of water or in a desert) often gives insight into how well someone feels cared for, nourished, how deeply rooted they are, and where they find rest.

Seasons can be a powerful metaphor. As we grow, we learn to accept that life has seasons, good and bad, with both blessings and struggles (typified as spring/summer or fall/winter). You can use this art activity to learn what season your counselee is in, and begin to build a picture of how they see their life and in what ways you can help them see the Lord in the midst of whatever season they are in.

Directions:

Using the idea of a tree as a metaphor, brainstorm all the features and traits of a tree. List with the young person all the various types of trees you can think of, along with where you find them, whether they produce any fruit or flowers, what seasons the trees thrive in or don't thrive in, etc.

Ask the counselee, "If you were a tree, what type of tree would you be?" Direct him or her to begin drawing himself or herself as a tree. Have the child consider what their surroundings would be, what season would they be in, and what else they would include in the picture that represents them. Would anyone or anything be in the picture with them? Would anything be in the tree?

Give them time to work on the tree, and tell them just to let you know when they are finished. Encourage them for the effort they put into the drawing. Ask them to share their drawing and why they picked certain details for their picture. What weaknesses or concerns do they identify? Take note of this, and ask them further questions.

Follow-up Questions:

- What tree did you pick for yourself? Why?
- How does it represent you?

- Is there anything in the tree or on the tree? What does it represent?
- What are your surroundings? Did you pick a specific environment? If so, why?
- Are you alone in the picture? If not, who or what else is there with you?
- What season do you think you are in and why?
- What is the weather like? Has it been like that for a long time? Do you think it will last?
- What would you want to change, if you could?
- What do you feel are the strengths about your picture? The strengths about you?

Things to Observe:

Look for how abstract or symbolic your counselee is in his or her self-expression. Are they quite literal and create a picture of a favorite tree in their backyard, offering little self-disclosure? Does the young person readily use this activity to make helpful connections to themselves and their personal situations? What concerns or goals do you identify?

Next: How do you move from gathering information about trees, environment, and seasons to discussing a counselee's real-life issues? It depends on what information you uncover as the project progresses. Does it give helpful insight into their circumstances or views? Are there ways you can speak in and give more clarity or accuracy? Are there misperceptions you need to gently correct or ways you can affirm what they see? Are there helpful goals you can develop for ministering to them?

This art activity could be paired well with "The Fruit Tree" activity on page 151 if it helps a young person to make connections to their choices, behaviors, and motivations of the heart.

Bridge Activity

What You Need:

> 12 x 18 paper or larger
> Various art mediums—crayons, colored pencils, markers, etc.

Goals:

Young people often reveal things about themselves when given an open-ended assignment like this. We want to see what they do with the directions, as well as enter in and guide them into fruitful conversation. This can move toward making goals and good choices—to consider choices or things they are walking away from or leaving behind, what they would like to move toward, and the steps they want to take to get there.

Directions/Follow-up Questions/Things to Observe:

Ask the young person to draw a bridge—any bridge they would like. Some will ask more questions about why they should draw a bridge, what type you are looking for, or if the bridge represents themselves. Explain that they can draw whatever they'd like and that there is no right or wrong way to do this activity. You want to observe how and what they draw. This will shape the questions you ask and what direction you will lead them in.

- Do they draw themselves in the picture?
- Are they on the bridge? What direction are they going?
- Is there anything under the bridge? What?
- What is the context, location, or background, if any?
- Does any of it have any meaning to them?

If you find that drawing a bridge took on meaning to them and leads your discussion in an obvious direction, feel free to adapt and go with what is helpful to them. If not, here are some follow-up ideas to gather information and develop meaningful rapport:

- If you were on the bridge, where would you be and why?
- What direction would you be going?
- Are you moving toward someone or something or away? What, or who?
- What are you looking forward to? What are you concerned about?
- Is anyone on the bridge with you?
- Are there steps we can come up with to help you grow, change, or make positive choices?

Boat and Refuge Activity

What You Need:

12 x 18 paper or larger

Various art mediums—crayons, colored pencils, markers, etc.

Goals:

This activity can be especially helpful for those who struggle with anxiety and fear. It is a setting for them to think about how their emotions and beliefs impact the way they look at life and where/how they find shelter.

Directions/Follow-up Questions/Things to Observe:

Ask the young person to draw a boat—any boat they would like—and ask him or her to draw what type of surroundings the boat is in. Explain that they can draw whatever they'd like, and that there is no right or wrong way to do this exercise.

After the child completes his or her picture, ask some of these questions:

- What type of boat did you draw, and why?
- Are you in the boat? Are you in the picture? Where?
- What else did you draw in the picture, and why?
- What type of body of water are you in? Why?
- Is the body of water calm or choppy or scary?
- What is the weather like? What season is it?
- Does anyone need rescued? If so, from what?
- How can help be given? And by whom?

Some children or teens will find this simply a fun activity, but complete it so quickly and on such a surface level that you aren't able to gather much helpful information. Other young people will reveal a great deal about themselves and their views of safety, stability, how they find rest, and how they view the Lord. Here are some additional questions to ask:

- If God were to enter into this situation, what would he look like?
- How would he come?
- Consider the following passages from the Psalms. What are some ways God is described? How does this help you when you are facing a big storm in your life?

Psalm 73:28: "But for me it is good to be near God; I have made the Lord God my refuge, that I may tell of all your works."

Psalm 62:7: "On God rests my salvation and my glory; my mighty rock, my refuge is God."

- What would it look like for God to be your refuge in this picture?
- What does it mean that the Lord is your rock?

Psalm 18:2: "The LORD is my rock and my fortress and my deliverer, my God, my rock, in whom I take refuge, my shield, and the horn of my salvation, my stronghold."

- If God entered into this picture, what would you draw?
- How would he help?
- How would he be your deliverer? Your shield?

Brainstorm with the teen or child and see what they can come up with. Look for ways you can help make connections for them when they are struggling to do so themselves. Then, consider how you can make those connections come to life in the actual places where they struggle. How can they trust God to be their deliverer, and what does that tangibly mean in their circumstances? What can and should they expect God to do or not do?

The Psalms are full of rich imagery for the ways God is their shield, protector, refuge, high tower, shelter, etc. Feel free to think winsomely and creatively for additional ways Scripture may speak to the child you are working with.

Door Activity

What You Need:

> Picture of a door
> 12 x 18 paper or larger
> Various art mediums—crayons, colored pencils, markers, etc.

Goals:

A picture of a door can represent anticipation—what lies on the other side of it? It can also represent either hopes and dreams, or fear and uncertainty about the future. For some, a door may even symbolize danger and enemies that lie in wait. On the contrary, a door could also symbolize an invitation to start something new and exciting. Whatever the metaphor, a picture of a door can be used to engage a child or teen to help discover what they imagine to be behind the door and why.

Directions:

You can choose to be nondirective in your approach. Say something like, "Here is a door. I want you to imagine what might be waiting for you on the other side. You can either write your thoughts and answers, or draw a picture. What would you prefer?" Or you could be more specific and directive, by saying something like, "I know you are worried about your senior year of high school. If you could imagine all the things waiting for you behind this door as you start school, good or bad, what might they be?"

After they write, draw, or otherwise interact with your question, be attentive to what they share and why. Much like the previous activities, how you address and speak into someone's life and circumstances will directly correspond with what you uncover and how you understand their need. You will want to consider how the gospel intersects with their experiences and how you can build bridges between the two.

Things to Observe:

Again, this resource can go in a multitude of directions. Ask the Lord for wisdom as you look for the themes that emerge. You will want to ask questions based on what the child or teen divulges. This will also require you to ask yourself how the Lord speaks to these issues and how you might begin to talk about this with the child. Look for:

- patterns, habits, or behaviors that need addressed.
- relational conflict that can be identified and worked on.
- strong fears or emotions you can follow up on and ask what informs them.
- places where they are excited, encouraged, and/or find hope.
- places where they are tempted to put too much hope or comfort.

Chapter 7

Activities for Drawing Out Children and Teens

UNDERSTANDING CHILDREN

In counseling we want to make sure we are committed to knowing others well. That means we are slow to jump to conclusions, and first demonstrating to them that they are heard and known. Proverbs 18:2 warns us, "A fool takes no pleasure in understanding, but only in expressing his opinion." May we never be people who delight in speaking too quickly and taking pleasure in expressing our own opinions. The love of God compels us to draw others out, listen well, understand as fully as possible, and then speak truth wisely.

This section is all about just that: thoughtfully drawing out kids and teens so we can know them well. Some activities draw out their feelings, some draw out their values, thoughts/beliefs, fears/anxieties, family dynamics, and circumstances. All of the activities, to some degree or another, draw out how they see their world.

The following was stated in the previous chapter, but it bears repeating. Always remember:

- You are adapting them to the child in front of you. Consider what you are hoping to learn about them.
- For the most part, each expressive activity can be modified to both elementary kids and teenagers; exceptions will be noted as needed.
- Take your time doing the activity. It is not an item to check off your list; there is no time frame. Your goal is building bridges of trust and relationship and opening doors to better know them in the future.

- It is good to stop and talk about things that come out while doing the activity. Don't simply focus on an end result (completing the task), but really invest in the process (learning, knowing and seeing the world through their eyes).

- It is often helpful to enlarge many of the images seen in this book so that young people have more room to work, color, or draw. Poster size is great to use with young people. They can also be laminated for use with dry erase markers. You can add VELCRO® strips to a laminated poster, as well as to butterflies, flies, hearts, dots, or any other creative item you'd like to use. Be creative. Please feel free to build on the activities, revamp them to fit the needs of your situation, and to even create your own.

UNDERSTANDING THEIR IDENTITY

Get to Know Me

What You Need:

Get to Know Me worksheet

Goals:

On the next page is a simple worksheet you can walk through with children when you first meet. It is a way to break the ice and ask both interesting and fun questions about who they are and what they like.

Directions:

You can hand this out before the child meets with you and let the child fill it out in his or her own words. Or, you can fill it out together, as a way to get to know the child. When filling it out, I will often take the time to ask follow-up questions and see if they will share more information about family, what school is like, who they are closest to, etc.

Follow-up Questions:

These will be tailored to the specific responses each young person gives.

GET TO KNOW ME

My name is:

I am (age):

I live with:

I go to _____ (school)
and I'm in _____ (grade).

My favorite subjects are:

My least favorite subjects are:

My favorite things to do:

My least favorite things to do:

I'm good at:

I'm not good at:

When I am all alone I think about:

I feel happy when:

I worry about:

I get sad when I think about:

I can share my feelings better when:

My favorite people to be with are:

It is hard spending time with:

I spend the most time with:

I like it when my family:

I don't like it when my family:

I don't like to tell others:

It is easy to talk to others when they:

I wish other people would:

My safe people are:

People who feel unsafe are:

I would describe God like this:

I feel close to God when:

I don't feel close to God when:

Colored Candy Activity

What You Need:

Candies, in a variety of colors

Goals:

This is a great get-to-know-you activity that can start the process of drawing out what a child thinks, feels, or how they see life. It can also be adapted to discuss one specific area of concern on a deeper level.

Directions:

Have a variety of colorful candy on hand. Try also to have more than one option, in case a child has a food allergy or doesn't like a specific kind of candy. Select a bag, dump out a pile of the candy in front of the child, and ask the child to help separate the candy by color. Explain that each pile of candy represents a subject they can tell you about. Ask what color they'd like to start with and give them the small pile of candy. Tell them what topic that color represents and ask them to tell you one thing (emotion or idea, for example, depending on the topic at hand). The child can then eat one piece of candy for each example shared. For instance, if I want to talk to a child about anger, I may choose a pile of red candy and say, "Tell me all the things that make you feel angry. You may eat a piece of candy for each one you tell me. Ready?"

Use this activity to draw out children's thoughts and feelings about each thing they share. Ask for examples, have them tell you a story, etc. If a child is sharing all the things that make him or her anxious, squeeze in more questions like: "Riding the bus makes you anxious? Why?" Wait for the answer. "Are there people on the bus who make you anxious? Who?" Wait for the answer. Then they might choose to go on to the next thing that makes them anxious. Once you are done, move to the next color/topic until you have run out of time or finished the candy.

If there is a specific topic you really want to encourage a child to talk about, choose the color with the most candy and use that color to represent the topic you want to learn about. This is particularly helpful for younger kids or those who need a little extra motivation to share.

This activity can be broad as mentioned above, or it can be made very specific to a topic you know or suspect the child is struggling with. Consider what kind of information you'd like to learn, and adapt the questions to your situation. The following are a few possible approaches/topics, and what the various colors of candy can represent:

Broad categories:
Blue—things that make you sad
Red—things that make you angry

Green—things that make you excited
Yellow—things that make you happy
Orange—things that make you upset
Brown—things that hurt you

Specific topic: Anger
Red—something that makes you angry
Brown—something you do when you are angry
Orange—a guess about why it makes you angry
Yellow—something you'd like to feel instead of anger
Green—something you could do differently when you're angry
Blue—something a person could do to help you

Things to Observe:

Again, customize the categories and questions based on what you are trying to encourage the child to talk about. Children will tend to be less resistant to discussing unpleasant topics when motivated by something enjoyable in the process. Before you know it, they are sharing things they might never have shared without an enjoyable diversion.

For example, if you want to instill problem-solving skills, perhaps make one pile of candy larger and call it, "kind responses you can say to your dad when you are angry," "things you could say to a bully," or "ways you can respond to fights with your sister."

Feel free to brainstorm with children when they get stuck. Perhaps they share a good idea and you can add some more suggestions or examples. Remember, these activities are meant to facilitate open conversation and change. The goal isn't to stick to a script or simply compete the task; it is to enter into their world, understand them, and help effect change.

If I Were a Superhero

What You Need:

If I Were a Superhero worksheet

Goals:

Superheroes have fostered tremendous inspiration and imagination in the lives of young people. There are many reasons that children and teens are drawn into a superhero story or movie. Superheroes possess larger-than-life capabilities, triumphantly rise above conflict and misfortune, give a sense of hope in the presence of tragedy, show courage in the face of oppression, and demonstrate good conquering evil. They provide examples of victors overcoming adversity and underdogs achieving the impossible. Because of this, superheroes can readily be used to connect with children in counseling.

Children become quickly attached to exciting rescue stories. These narratives can provide an avenue for children and teens to use their imagination to bring their own stories and uniqueness to life.

Directions:

Talk through each question one by one. As the child answers them, feel free to ask follow-up questions and enter into a discussion about why the child answered the way he or she did. Often one question can lead you into meaningful conversation that says a lot about how the child thinks, feels, and perceives life.

Follow-up questions will flow out of the answers you are given. Does the child feel they have enemies? If so, why? What makes for an enemy? If the child identifies a weakness, does it parallel a struggle or weakness in their real life or is it imagined?

Observations:

In an activity like this, you are looking for ways the answers reflect the child's perceptions, fears, insecurities, worries, and desires. Is there a longing for a partner and relationships, or do they express a desire for isolation? What does the desired superpower say about them? Is there any correlation to what is occurring in their lives or struggles?

Where there are clear connections to what is going on in the child's life, you will want to consider how can use that in speaking back into their struggle. This takes thoughtfulness, imagination and wisdom to find the biblical truths. Creatively framing the conversation around their enjoyment of superheroes will serve to engage them well.

IF I WERE A SUPERHERO

If a were a superhero, I'd be:

My superhero powers would be:

My weaknesses would be:

My enemy would be:

Because:

My superhero costume would be:

My superhero hideout would be:

My partner would be:

He or she would help me in this way:

My Timeline

What You Need:

My Timeline worksheet and pen or pencil

Goals:

This activity can be a helpful way for you to build a timeline of life events, good or bad, that have impacted the child or teen you are working with. You can help a child or teen map important events chronologically to get a bird's-eye view of their lives. Talking through the major events in their lives on a year-by-year (or event-by-event) basis will help you gather important details and see an accurate order of events.

Directions:

Ask the child to share his or her happiest moments on the top of the timeline and his or her hardest life events on the bottom of the timeline. You can fill out the sheet as they are telling their story to you. Sometimes older kids might want to be the ones to write it down, but my experience is that it slows down conversation; most are happier to allow you to be the "secretary" for them.

When possible, it is also helpful to give parents a copy and ask them to write out what they see as impactful events in their child's life, while you complete a separate worksheet with the child or teen. This will give you an opportunity to compare what each party wrote. It always helps to have both a parent's perspective and the child's point of view. It helps you evaluate the child's recollection of events and confirm facts. It also provides a picture of how events unfolded and often helps the young person to step back and see his or her life in an orderly manner.

Follow-up Questions:

- Is there anything that surprises you, or that you think is interesting about your timeline?
- If you could add or take away anything that has happened, what would it be?

Things to Observe:

As you review the young person's completed timeline, are positive or negative events clustered together or spread out? Was there a particular year or two that affected them more deeply than others? How did it impact them developmentally? Who helped them process or respond to these events?

When possible and with permission, I like to share the timeline with a parent to gather their observations. It might be possible that a child has confused dates or events. It might also be helpful to have a parent add other significant events they feel the child has hidden, simply is unaware of, or has forgotten. It is also possible to invite the parent to observe and participate, when beneficial.

MY TIMELINE

by _____
(your name here)

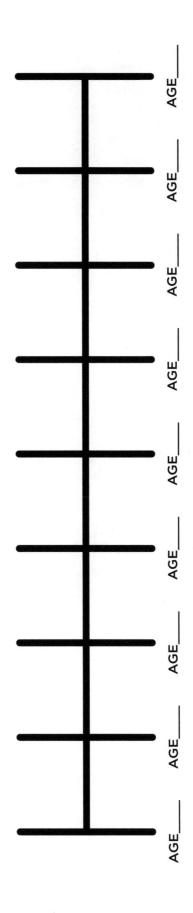

AGE____ AGE____ AGE____ AGE____ AGE____ AGE____ AGE____ AGE____

Questions for Teens

What You Need:

Questions for Teens worksheet
Writing instrument

Goals:

Gather information about the teen's views, likes, dislikes, and perceptions.

Directions:

This can be filled out by a teen before the two of you meet. It can also be filled out when first getting to know the teen, or sent home as an assignment.

Follow-up Questions:

No follow-up questions are needed, unless the teen says something you feel needs a follow-up discussion.

Things to Observe:

- How short or long are the teen's answers?
- Does he/she open up and share, or are answers closed-off and unrevealing?
- Do any significant themes or patterns emerge from the answers?
- Is anything disturbing or alarming revealed?
- Does the teen have healthy relationships in his/her life?
- Does he/she have any destructive relationships?

This information should provide a jumping-off point in order to dig deeper in getting to know a teenager. Where does the teen seem well-adjusted and mature? Where does he or she seem to be wrestling with something, hiding something, or thinking unwisely? How can you approach talking about this further?

QUESTIONS FOR TEENS

1. What are your goals for your life? What do you hope to accomplish or have?

2. What do you put your hope in?

3. What are the things you worry about or fear?

4. When you get overwhelmed with grief or hurt, what do you feel like doing?

5. What do you think you need?

6. What would make you feel better in your grief or fear?

7. What things or ways do you look to, in order to have your needs met?

8. Does performance matter to you? Why or why not?

9. Does what people think matter to you? Why or why not?

10. Whose opinion or approval is most important to you? Why?

11. Who or what are your role models?

12. What gives your life meaning?

13. On your deathbed, what would sum up your life as worthwhile?

14. How do you define success?

15. How do you define failure?

16. What makes you feel secure?

17. What things do you treasure?

18. What things do you pray for?

19. How do you spend your free time? What do you like to do?

20. How would you complete the thought, "If only . . ."?

21. Where do you find your identity? How do you define who you are?

If I Were a . . .

What You Need:

"If I Were a . . ." worksheet
Writing instrument

Goals:

The goal is to gather information about the child in a creative way. It is a projective exercise to see how children perceive themselves and why. It will often reveal if they lean toward being abstract or concrete and how active their imagination is.

Directions:

Let them fill out the questions, or offer to be their "secretary" and write down their answers for them. Remember, children will often write as little as possible, whereas you want to gather as much information as possible. Any time you can do the writing for them, they will likely have more to say, and you will have documented their thoughts and ideas more thoroughly.

Follow-up Questions:

You may simply want to expound upon what they say by asking deeper questions, such as:
- What do you like about being that type of [tree, animal, color]?
- Why does that season make you [happy, sad, afraid]?

Things to Observe:

Developmentally, you will want to observe how easy or hard this activity is for children.

You are looking to see how vivid their imagination is (or isn't). Are they self-revealing, or self-protective? Do they become silly, and their responses have no meaning? Do they think deeply and demonstrate extraordinary insightfulness?

"IF I WERE A . . ."

If I were a tree, I'd be a:
Because:

If I were a color, I'd be:
Because:

If I were an animal, I'd be:
Because:

If I were a toy, I'd be a:
Because:

If I were a superhero, I'd be:
Because:

If I were a famous person, I'd be:
Because:

If I could live in any season, I'd live in: Fall   Winter   Spring   Summer
Because:

If I were a bug, I'd be a:
Because:

If I were a type of vehicle, I'd be a:
Because:

If I were a character from a fairy tale, I'd be:
Because:

UNDERSTANDING THEIR EMOTIONS

What Are You Feeling?

Things You Need:

- A variety of coloring options, if possible: crayons, colored pencils, small tip markers, etc. However, if you only have one option available, make sure children are given a wide variety of colors to work with.
- What Are You Feeling? worksheet
- The Person (or Heart) Outline (In the following pages you will see this person outline used for various expressive activities. It can be used as a black and white or a colorized copy. See page 199 for instructions on how to access colorized files of all graphics for this book.)
- Emotions Chart. This tool can help for kids or teens who get stuck (or need prompting) thinking about what emotions they feel. Have them identify which emotions they most relate to.

Goals:

- Information-gathering activity for teens and children, designed to help explore and evaluate a child's emotions
- To identify the emotions a child/teen feels most often and how those emotions are experienced
- To help the child or teen have a greater self-awareness of his or her feelings
- To identify problematic emotions that may need help/intervention
- To establish goals for helping the child work through negative or destructive emotions

Directions:

It is important to do this activity in steps:

1) We all have things we feel. Using the "What Are You Feeling?" circles page, ask, "What do you think are the six emotions you feel most often? I want you to write (or, I can write for you) one emotion in each circle."

2) Start with the first circle. Say, "Tell me what emotion you picked." (For example, the child might pick "anger.") Now ask, "What kind of things make you feel (anger)? I'm going to be your secretary and write down what you tell me." When the child is finished, ask "What else?" Continue asking until the child says he or she is done. You always want to assume that children have more to share until they tell you they do not. Do this with each circle/emotion and write down what they say next to each circle.

3) Once you are done, say you'd like him/her to pick a color that best represents the emotion and to color in the circle with that color. Have the child do this with each circle, and leave out each colored pencil or crayon so he or she can use it again. After the child is done, go back and ask what color he/she picked for each circle and why. Have him/her tell you the color rather than you assuming the color. For example, red could be a berry color because it reminds the child of strawberries that make her happy, or blue could be light blue to him for tears/sadness. Give children the opportunity to nuance their answers if they want. Some will just say, "Brown, because it seems like a brown emotion." Record next to each circle what they say.

4) Have them take each color they picked for their emotions and color the outline of their body (supplied on page 95) in all the places where they feel that emotion. When they finish, have them tell you about the picture, where they placed the emotion in the body, and why. Record what they say on the same piece of paper.

This activity can also be done with the outline of a heart (also supplied on page 96). You can ask, "Color into your heart where you think you feel emotions and how much you feel them." For most kids, the bigger/stronger the emotion, the more room it will take in the heart. The heart gives you an idea what they feel the strongest and how often. The outline of the body gives you an idea how it might come out in their actions or behavior.

Follow-up Questions:

You always want to adapt your language, directions, and follow-up questions to the developmental level of the child or teen you are working with. Also note that this activity can be done one-on-one, in a family context, or in a group context. Sharing in small groups can help teens feel they are not alone in their struggles with various emotions and help facilitate healthy discussions about how to deal with them.

Things to Observe:

Doing this activity can provide you with various insights. First, notice how children respond to an activity like this. What does it say about where they are developmentally or emotionally? Do they enjoy coloring, or dislike it? Is their work neat and organized, or messy and disorganized? Do they take a long time deciding and thinking, or do they rush and move quickly? Do they struggle expressing emotion? Do they struggle picking or identifying emotions?

Second, you want to better understand what situations create those emotions. What makes them happy? sad? angry? afraid? nervous? bored? Does it reveal relational struggles at home or with others? Does it reveal internal struggles? Are the emotions they picked more negative? positive? balanced? If so, why? How do children/teens perceive their lives or themselves?

Third, establish an idea of what the child may need help with, what you might help foster/encourage in them, and what needs to change. This could be shared with a parent to gather their input as well: What surprises them? What do they validate? What would they add from their perspective?

Additional Suggestion for Younger Children:

If a child is younger and doesn't yet understand the concept of emotions and colors, you can use books to help build their understanding. Dr. Seuss's *My Many Colored Days* is a great book to read out loud before starting the activity, in order to build a picture of what they are to do in the activity.[8] Warning: some children will try to mimic the emotions and ideas in the book, so you will want to emphasize the need to think through what emotions they feel most often.

You can ask follow-up questions for establishing goals or first steps, such as:

- Number the emotions from 1–6 in order of how often you feel them. Which do you feel most? Which do you feel least?
- If you could get rid of any of these emotions or replace them, which would you replace? Put a star next to them. What would you put in their place? Use the emotions chart if you need to.
- What emotions would you want to keep? Why?

Thoughtfully consider how this information helps you understand the child before you. What does it tell you about them emotionally? How do they tend to express, handle, and manage their emotions? Do they struggle expressing them?

You can also do this activity with a more specific goal, saying something like "Tell me what emotions you feel most often when your family fights," or "What are the six emotions you feel most often about your [parents' divorce]?" You might also revisit this activity at a later time, to see how much progress has been made.

WHAT ARE YOU FEELING?

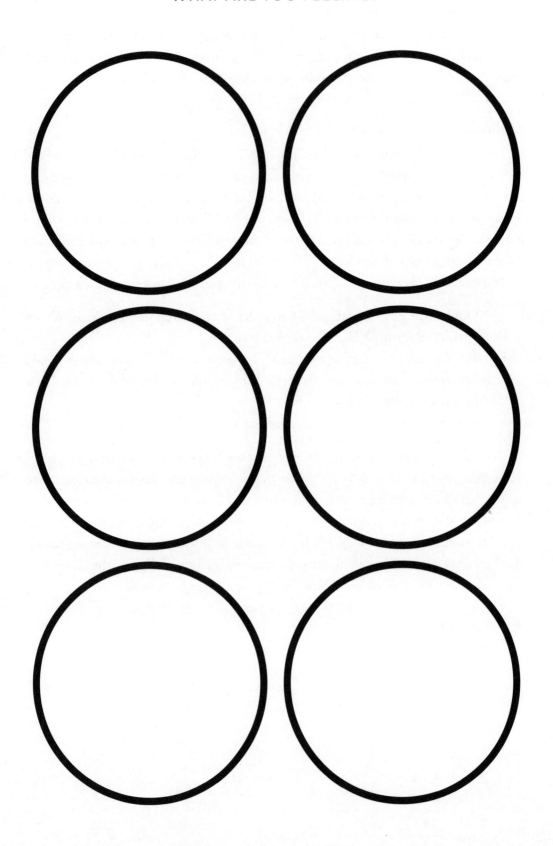

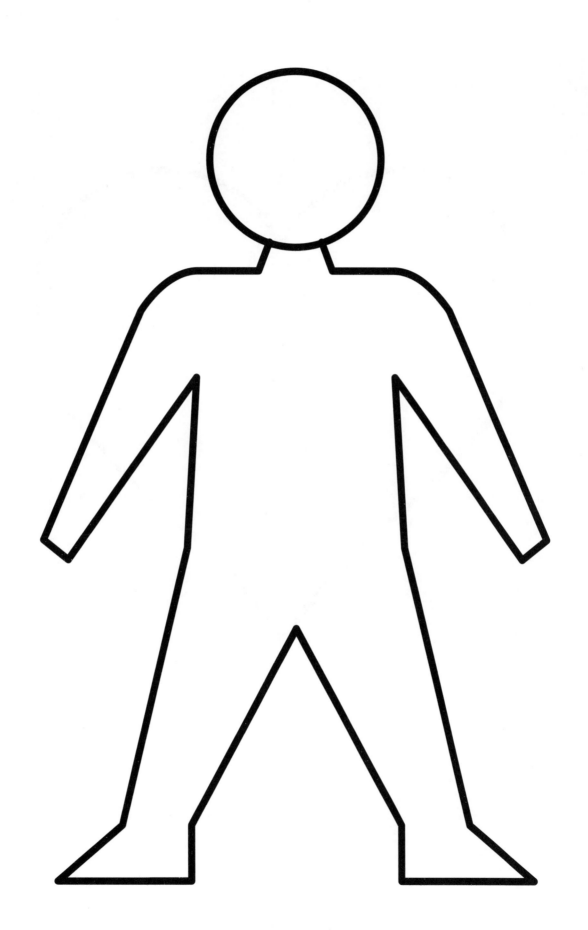

EMOTIONS CHART

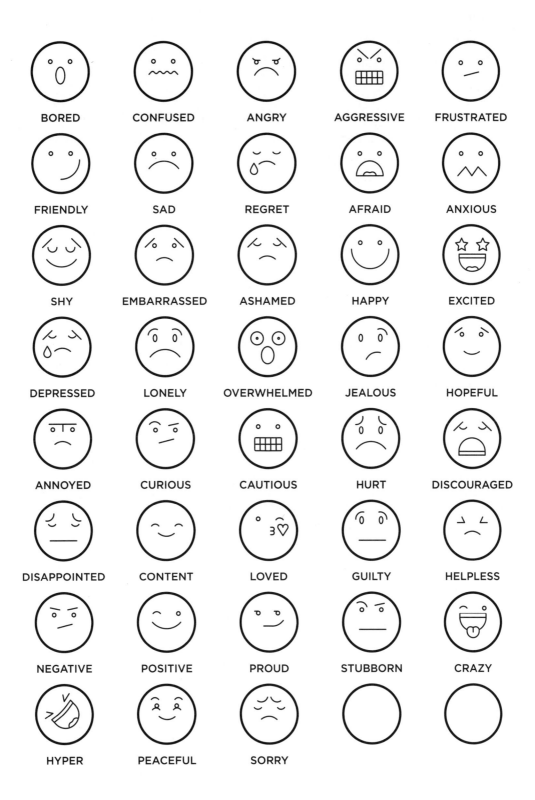

Measure Your Feelings

What You Need:

Several copies of the Measure Your Feelings worksheet
Any writing or coloring instrument

Goals:

Young people can have big feelings/emotions—anger, sadness, fear, anxiety, etc.—and for various reasons. It can help kids to self-reflect on how often and how strongly they feel such emotions during the week.

Having kids fill in and measure how they are feeling during the course of the week can do several things:

- Help you see how strong their emotions are
- Help identify patterns—specific days when emotions are higher or lower, and possible stressors that cause them
- Help you or parents better prepare and respond to emotions/hard days and what leads to them
- Help kids make connections and see patterns or reasons they are struggling
- Can be used initially as a regular check-in, or as a way to demonstrate progress/growth

Directions:

Discuss how our feelings sometimes fluctuate from week to week and depending on what might be going on in a given day. If there is a specific emotion a child struggles with, explain that you would like him or her to keep track of how strong that emotion or reaction is each day for the next week or two. (You will probably need to make copies of the "rulers" worksheet.)

At the end of each day, the child should fill out or color the worksheet, indicating how strong/severe the struggles (anxiety, frustration, sadness, etc.) were that day. Perhaps parents will want to track how reactive, compliant, or willful their child is. The sheet could be used to measure a number of feelings or reactions, based on the counseling goals.

Ask the child and parent to talk about what made it a better or harder day, and to take notes or write comments on the side of their worksheets. This way, when they bring the worksheets back to you, they have reminders of what happened each day.

Follow-up Questions:

Have the family or teen bring their worksheets back in, and then discuss why they filled it out the way they did.

- Was there anything in particular that stood out?
- What made it better or worse?
- Were there themes to what days or times things became harder for them?
- How did they handle the moments that were hard?

Things to Observe:

Watch if there are particular days or times of the week when the young person tends to do better or worse. Look for patterns or clues as to what makes them react the way they do.

Doing this for many weeks can inform how and why they are emotional or reactive, and also gives them a visual for whether they are doing well or not. This can be a helpful motivation to encourage proactively working on the source of struggle.

MEASURE YOUR FEELINGS OF

MONDAY
0 1 2 3 4 5 6

TUESDAY
0 1 2 3 4 5 6

WEDNESDAY
0 1 2 3 4 5 6

THURSDAY
0 1 2 3 4 5 6

FRIDAY
0 1 2 3 4 5 6

SATURDAY
0 1 2 3 4 5 6

SUNDAY
0 1 2 3 4 5 6

What's Bugging You?

What You Need:

Person outline (see page 95)

Stickers of bugs

Writing utensils including pen, pencil, colored pencils, or markers

Goals:

Use the bug stickers to get a picture of all the things that "bug," bother, or frustrate children you are counseling. Depending on how open-ended you make the activity, a child may interpret this exercise in many different ways; however, all interpretations are beneficial to helping you better understand them. If you want very specific information, you can be more precise in what you ask them to represent. For example, you can direct them to the supplies and tell them, "I want to know all the things that bug you or make you frustrated about school"; "I want to know all the things that bug you about your brothers and sisters"; or, "I want to brainstorm all the things that bug you about having a disability."

No matter the specific topic at hand, having children brainstorm all the details they can think of frees them from the pressure of only having one "right" answer. It allows them to express a variety and complexity of thoughts and ideas.

This activity can be effective with any age, though older teens may rebuff it at first. However, for an older teen who struggles to communicate, or is very guarded or withdrawn, this would be a helpful tool. This could be a good group activity to do as well, either with a family, small group, or youth group.

Directions:

Pull out the person outline, and then explain to children that you want them to brainstorm all the things that bug them. Hand them the stickers and tell them they can place a sticker wherever they want, then tell you something that "bugs" or bothers them. You will be their secretary and write down what they say.

After each sticker, feel free to ask follow-up questions or allow them to tell stories to illustrate their point. This gives you the opportunity to hear how they think and interpret situations, and helps build trust. After each example, ask, "What else?" or "What's next?" Assume they have more to tell you until they tell you they are finished.

When they let you know they are finished, have them look over their project (along with your notes) and ask if there is anything they'd like to add or change, to make sure they are satisfied with the picture.

Follow-up Questions:

- Ask the child to circle the top three irritants that bug them most. This will help you discern what factors cause the most frustration, and can establish a starting point and goals for your time together. Often I will ask, "Would it be OK if you and I work on these things first and talk about ways we can help you?"
- Ask what the two or three factors are that bother them least. This will show you which details are more peripheral to the child's situation.
- Sometimes, if a child is struggling to identify how he or she feels, you can invite a parent into the discussion and offer to let the parent brainstorm with them.

Things to Observe:

When you give children the freedom to place the stickers wherever they want, you will sometimes notice them placing stickers in places on the body picture to represent their struggle (e.g., a sticker is put on a leg because they are "bad at running," or a sticker is placed on the head because "classmates tell me I'm dumb").

There will often be themes that emerge from this activity: family struggles, identity issues, bullying troubles, etc., so observe how the pertinent details may be connected and why.

Butterflies in My Belly

What You Need:

> Person outline (see page 95)
> Sheet of butterfly stickers
> Pens or colored pencils

Goals:

This is a brainstorming activity to draw out what makes a young person anxious. You want to help children or teens share all the things that give them anxiety, fear, or apprehension.

This exercise can also be done in a small group or family context as well. Sometimes it helps to hear how others struggle and what they do when they are anxious. It may help a child or teen feel like they are not alone, or others have similar struggles. It can also help facilitate discussion and encouragement.

Directions:

Hand children a person outline and a sheet of butterfly stickers. Explain that sometimes when we feel anxious or afraid, we call it "butterflies in our belly." Ask them if they ever feel that way. Explain that you want to brainstorm some of the things that might make them feel anxious inside. They can stick a butterfly anywhere they want on the page and then tell you something that makes them feel anxious, worried, or fearful. You will be their secretary and write down what they have to say.

Use their words and descriptions as much as possible when taking notes. Encourage as much conversation as they are comfortable with. Ask questions like, "Can you give me an example?" or What makes you feel this way? This helps you better understand their experiences and perceptions. After each sticker, ask "What else?" or "What's next?" Always assume they have more to share until they tell you they are finished. When they have finished sharing, ask if there is anything they'd like to change or add to their picture.

Follow-up Questions:

- What are the top three things you worry about most? Circle them.
- What are the two that you worry about least? Underline them.
- Is there one thing you'd be willing to talk about first and we can work on together? Put a star next to that one.
- Are there butterflies you'd want to get rid of? Are there butterflies you wouldn't want to lose? Why?

Things to Observe:

- Where did children place the stickers? Do you see any patterns?
- What things they are anxious about? Do you see any themes?
- If the parents are present or able to look over the activity, would there be anything they would add? Is there anything that surprises them about how their children completed the activity?

UNDERSTANDING THEIR HEART

What's Going On in Your Heart?

This is a resource to use to help illustrate to young people what's going on inside of them. Children often connect with illustrations; when they can't put their finger on what's going on, they can often point to a picture that captures what they feel inside.

For a child that struggles with the ability to articulate what is going on inside, it can help prompt them. You can walk through each picture and discuss what might make one feel "peaceful" or "proud" or "insecure." This may foster openness about times they have felt the same way.

It can be laminated, blown up as a poster, or remain in a book for a reference. If you work with children or teens regularly, it is a helpful poster to function as a discussion starter.

WHAT'S GOING ON IN YOUR HEART?

ANGRY   INSECURE   FULL OF FAITH   TRUSTING

GUILTY   UNBELIEVING   DISCOURAGED   STUBBORN

PEACEFUL   THANKFUL   ANXIOUS   HOPEFUL

WISE   PROUD   LOVING   JEALOUS

PRAYERFUL   APATHETIC   SELFISH   CONFUSED

FOOLISH   GIVING   ASHAMED   CONTENT

Heart Puzzle

What You Need:

Heart Outline (see page 96) or Heart Puzzle (page 108)
Colorful writing instruments, including crayons, colored pencils, markers, etc.

Goals:

This can be used with parents, children, or teens to help them gather a better picture of how and what the child feels. Often, it can be helpful to look at all the things a child thinks or feels as if it were a puzzle. There can be a variety of pieces, and we are striving to understand how they are fit together. It can be beneficial in helping young people better understand themselves.

Directions:

Sit down with children or teens and brainstorm how God has created feelings. Start with the things they know they feel often and write one in each puzzle piece. Some kids can fill in the whole heart, while some may struggle to figure out what they feel and need prompting to think about it. Sometimes those things become clear in time; sometimes we need help/wisdom to understand what fits together and where.

Follow-up Questions:

- What emotions do you think you feel most often?
- What feelings do you think you feel strongest?
- What are all the things you think are going on in your heart?
- What are your strongest feelings when you're at school?
- What are the strongest feelings when you're at home?
- What emotions do you like most? Star them.
- What emotions do you like least? Or what emotions would you want to change? Put a box around them.
- What emotions do you feel for the longest amount of time? Why do you think that is?

If a child is going through a loss, divorce, or some other kind of hard time, you could ask more specific questions like, "What are the emotions you felt when [you lost your dad in the car accident]?" or "What feelings did you have when you were cyberbullied?"

Things to Observe:

Does the young person struggle to express himself or herself? Is it because it is too painful, because he/she is disinterested, or because he/she is confused about what to do? Look for places where you see growth and maturity, as well as for any deficits or concerns.

This activity could be shared with a parent to help provide input or insight, if helpful.

HEART PUZZLE

Stars and Dots

What You Need:

Person outline (see page 95); a figure with skin tones would also be helpful for this activity

You Are Special, by Max Lucado[9]

Star stickers

Dot stickers

Pencil or colored pencil

Goals:

In the book *You Are Special,* there live small wooden people called Wemmicks. Every day they stick either gold stars or gray dots on one another, signifying approval or disapproval of the other people around them. The pretty, talented, and popular Wemmicks are always given stars. Other Wemmicks, however—the ones who can't do much or have chipped paint—are frowned at and given ugly gray dots. In this story Eli, the woodcarver/creator of the Wemmicks, helps one of his wooden creations understand how special he is—no matter what other Wemmicks may think. This story illustrates a fundamental lesson for readers that regardless of how the others value them, God treasures each of them, for he is their Designer and Creator.

The activity is easily accessible for children 5–14 years old. However, adults have expressed how helpful this story and imagery has been to them.

Directions:

Read the book to the young person. Feel free to stop and talk about the story, the characters, or particular statements the characters make. Ask the child if he or she has ever felt like one of the wooden people and why.

After reading the book, direct the child to the supplies. Give the child the star stickers and ask, "What are the stars you think people try to give you?" Brainstorm all the things people have praised the child for. Offer to be the child's "secretary" and write statements down while he/she sticks the stickers on the outline. Then ask, "What are the dots you think people try to give you?" Have the child place stickers and share where he/she feels criticized, snubbed, or looked down on. Write down what the child says.

Follow-up Questions:

- What would it mean to "not let the stickers stick"? Does it mean we shouldn't see our strengths or weaknesses, or does it mean we do not let those things determine our value?

- What stickers would you like to start getting rid of? (You can then help the child understand what the above passages mean and how to let go of the stars and dots the more he/she trusts in God's love.)
- What stickers are you tempted to keep? (Meaning: The child wants to find value in a certain star or dot.)

Things to Observe:

Children tend to answer the questions in two ways—either they express things they feel others like or dislike about them, or they express the things they like or dislike about themselves. Regardless of the way they answer, it is helpful to find out how they view themselves. Consider:

- Are there more stars or dots on the picture? What does this tell you? Does the child have a more negative or positive view of himself/herself?
- You can also review this with a parent and see what details surprise them, what specifics they can confirm, or what factors they thought would be included in the discussion but weren't.

This is also a great activity to use to speak back into the child's world. The point of the book is that "the stickers only stick if you let them." The more we trust in God's love for us and find value in him, the less we care what others say—*good or bad.*

We want to help children realize that their value isn't in their talents (or lack thereof), their looks, or what others around them think about them. They are uniquely and wonderfully made the way God wanted them to be.

Point kids to what God has to say about where their identity comes from. Opening a Bible or reading together is helpful. I like to print out a passage from the computer so we can read it together, highlight certain words, and draw connections. Here are several Scripture passages that speak to this:

- Jeremiah 1:5: "Before I formed you in the womb I knew you, and before you were born I consecrated you."
- Psalm 139:14: "I praise you, for I am fearfully and wonderfully made, Wonderful are your works; my soul knows it very well."
- 1 Peter 2:9: "But you are a chosen race, a royal priesthood, a holy nation, a people for his own possession, that you may proclaim the excellencies of him who called you out of darkness into his marvelous light."
- 1 John 3:1–2: "See what kind of love the Father has given to us, that we should be called children of God; and so we are. The reason why the world does not know us is that it did not know him. Beloved, we are God's children now, and what we will be has not yet appeared; but we know that when he appears we shall be like him, because we shall see him as he is."

UNDERSTANDING THEIR RELATIONSHIPS

Relational Assessment

What You Need:

Relational Assessment worksheet
Various colorful pens or colored pencils
Stickers (optional, but especially useful for younger children)

Goals:

- Build trust and rapport
- Gather information about the child's perception of personal relationships
- Discern where there are positive, supportive relationships and where there are negative relationships
- Build a working relationship with the child

Directions:

As you work through this activity, be mindful to give the child adequate time to complete each step. Do not ask any detailed questions until the child is completely finished writing.

To begin, give the child the Relational Assessment worksheet and explain the activity. Say something like the following, as you work through each of the boxes:

> *Let's talk today about the people who are in your life. I want you to pick a pen. What color would you like?*
>
> *In the center box, write your name. What do people call you?*
>
> *Who do you feel closest to? In the next box, I want you to put the names of the person (or people) that you feel closest to.*
>
> *Now, in the next box, I want you to put the people that you like and enjoy being with, but don't feel quite so close to. What are their names?*
>
> *Now, please write down the names of people who are a part of your life, but you don't feel close to.*
>
> *In the last box, list the people who are a part of your life but you don't like them, or perhaps have a hard time getting along with—maybe even someone who does things that hurt or even frighten you.*

When finished, have the child pick a different colored pen/pencil. Ask them:

> *Out of all the people you wrote down, who do you go to when you need help? Circle the names of those people.*

Who do you spend the most time with? Underline the names of those people.

Think about all the people you wrote down. Put a star next to the people you like best.

Who are the people you have a hard time getting along with? Put a box around those people.

If the child hasn't mentioned God, ask: "Where would you place God?"

For younger children, or for those with reading or writing difficulties, you may offer to write for them.

You may also use stickers and have the child (even teens) pick a sticker to represent each person identified, including themselves. It's best to offer a wide variety of stickers (animals, shapes, bugs, people, objects, etc.). This will give additional information regarding how the child sees each person. When you discuss the worksheet, be sure to ask the child what sticker was picked and why. Ask how the sticker represents the person. Always allow the child to tell you what the sticker is (even if it seems obvious). Children will often have specific reasons or names for their choices that can be revealing.

Follow-up Questions:

When the child is done, explore the details. Begin with the box closest to the center and ask whose name is in the box. Feel free to ask questions about each person (type of relationship, what makes it close, etc.). Then move on to each of the other boxes. Ask who is underlined, boxed, starred, or circled. Slowly and methodically, ask why the child made each of the choices shown.

You may also add or subtract questions, depending on what you know about the child's situation. Using different color highlighters, ask the child to answer questions such as:

- Who are the people who feel safe?
- Who are the people who feel unsafe?
- Who are the people who make you feel sad, happy, frustrated, angry, etc.?
- Who do you wish you could spend more time with?
- Is there anyone you wish were *not* in the picture?

Things to Observe:

This is your opportunity to learn more about the child's world. In all this, you are seeking to understand the quality of the child's relationships: Good? Bad? Indifferent? Constructive? Destructive? Isolated?

- How much or how little support is available in this child's life? Are there many names, only a few, or none?
- Who does the child talk to or go to for help?
- Are family members shown? How are they perceived?
- Does the child have many friends?
- Are there many difficult relationships? One particularly difficult relationship? What makes these relationships difficult?
- Does the child feel enjoyed and loved by anyone?
- Does the child spend a great amount of time with the people identified as easy to get along with, or is much time spent with people the child does not enjoy?
- Is God in the sphere of relationships? How does the child see God? Jesus? What is the quality of the relationship?

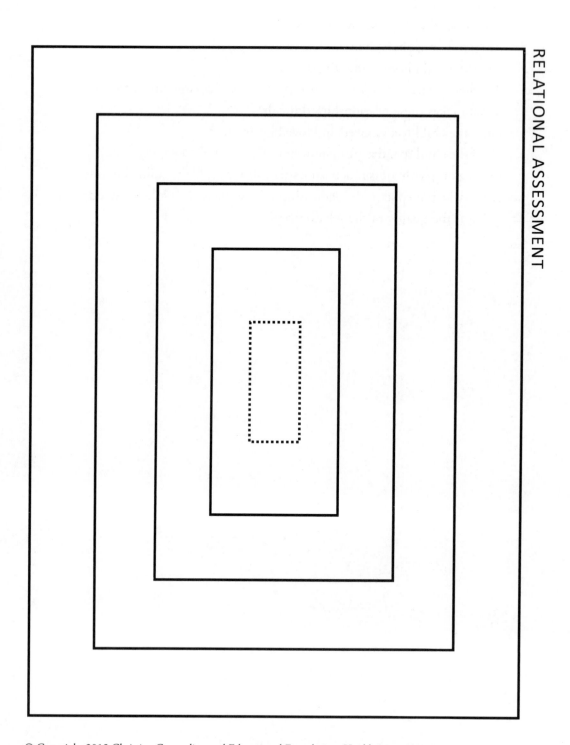

Care Tag

What You Need:

Blank care tag worksheet

Pen or pencil

Goals:

Many children and teens wish they were better understood by their family, peers, or the world around them. This activity helps draw out where they might feel misunderstood, as well as ways they'd like to be treated. This activity works well with ages six and up, but is especially helpful with older children and teens. It can also be valuable in a group setting, to facilitate conversation.

Directions:

Give a blank care tag worksheet to the young person. Explain that many items, particularly our clothes, come with tags that instruct us on how to properly care for the item. They will say things like, "Hand wash," "Handle with care," or "Dry flat."

Say, "Wouldn't it be nice if we came with care tags that helped us know how to treat others, or helped others know how to treat us? If you came with a care tag, what would you want yours to say? Write down what you'd want others to know about you."

Encourage the young person to write as much as possible. You can also be more specific in your instruction if you know there are places or relationships where the young person faces struggles. You could say, "If your parents could read your care tag, what would you want it to say?" Or, "If you could come up with a care tag for your friends to read, what would you want it to say?"

Follow-up Questions:

- Discuss with the young person what prompted the responses on the care tag.
- Does anyone care for you well? In what way?
- Who do they wish would care for you better? Why?
- Is how you desire to be cared for healthy or unhealthy? Reasonable or unwise?
- Is this how the Lord cares for you? Why or why not?

Things to Observe:

Take the discussion further, by explaining that God has given us a manual on how to care for others and how we should be cared for. Begin to discuss the ways Christ modeled to us how to care for one another. How does that inform our relationships now?

Below are a list of passages you can weave into your discussion. These help set a better standard of care for ourselves. You can read them, choose passages that speak directly to an issue that came from their care tag, or walk through what a healthy, godly view of care should be.

- Matthew 7:12 (NIV): "So in everything, do to others what you would have them do to you, for this sums up the Law and the Prophets."
- Matthew 22:39: "And a second is like it: You shall love your neighbor as yourself."
- Matthew 25:40: "And the King will answer them, 'Truly, I say to you, as you did it to one of the least of these my brothers, you did it to me.'"
- Luke 6:27: "But I say to you who hear, Love your enemies, do good to those who hate you."
- John 13:34–35 (NIV): "A new command I give you: Love one another. As I have loved you, so you must love one another. By this everyone will know that you are my disciples, if you love one another."
- Romans 13:8: "Owe no one anything, except to love each other, for the one who loves another has fulfilled the law."
- 1 Corinthians 13:4–7 (NIV): "Love is patient, love is kind. It does not envy, it does not boast, it is not proud. It does not dishonor others, it is not self-seeking, it is not easily angered, it keeps no record of wrongs. Love does not delight in evil but rejoices with the truth. It always protects, always trusts, always hopes, always perseveres."
- Ephesians 5:21: "submitting to one another out of reverence for Christ."
- Philippians 2:3 (NIV): "Do nothing out of selfish ambition or vain conceit. Rather, in humility value others above yourselves."
- Colossians 3:13 (NIV): "Bear with each other and forgive one another if any of you has a grievance against someone. Forgive as the Lord forgave you."
- 1 Thessalonians 5:12–13 (NIV): "Now we ask you, brothers and sisters, to acknowledge those who work hard among you, who care for you in the Lord and who admonish you. Hold them in the highest regard in love because of their work. Live in peace with each other."
- 1 Timothy 5:1–2: "Do not rebuke an older man but encourage him as you would a father, younger men as brothers, older women as mothers, younger women as sisters, in all purity."

CARE TAG

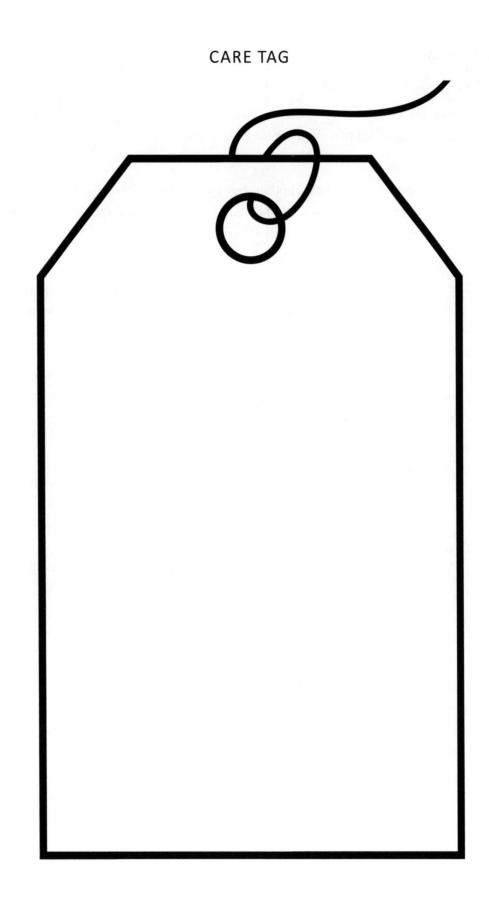

Walk in My Shoes

What You Need:

Shoe outlines worksheet (optional)

Pens, pencil, colored pencils, markers, or crayons

Goals:

This is a good activity to help children feel you understand what it is like to walk in their shoes. This can be particularly helpful for those who feel different than their peers, have been bullied, or wrestle with a disability.

Directions:

Have children roughly trace the outline of their feet on one piece of paper, or use the attached outline. Use this to get them talking about what it is like to be them, and how they deal with the things they struggle with.

Brainstorm all the things they feel make them who they are, what they wish others understood about them, or ways they feel others do not understand them. Ask them to tell you what it is like to "walk in their shoes," and let them write down all the things they can come up with.

Follow-up Questions:

Ask them to share what they wrote.

- How do you feel different from others?
- How do you feel alike?
- Who do you think understands you well?
- Who do you think does not? What might help them know and understand you better?

Additional Suggestion:

This activity can also be used with siblings and the whole family. Have everyone trace their feet, put their names at the top of the paper, then switch with one another. Each person writes what it must feel like to be the other person, or reads out loud what each family member wrote on their own shoe.

Encourage each person to share about themselves and what it is like to be in their world.

WALK IN MY SHOES

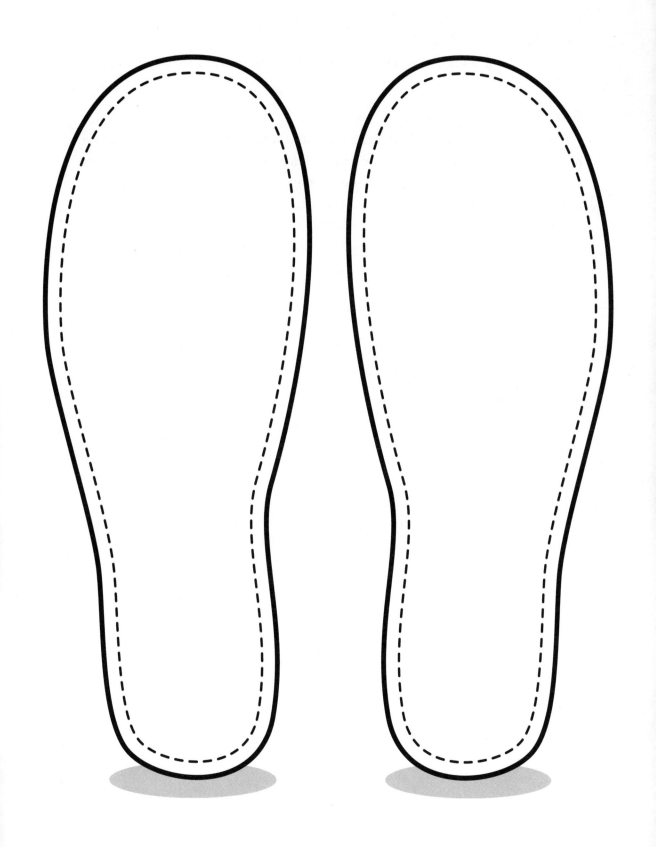

UNDERSTANDING THEIR CHALLENGES

How Big Is My Struggle?

This a resource that can be used at any age and with many of the activities in this book.

Goal:

Young people can identify with emotions and pictures more readily than they can put words to what they feel and how strongly they feel. Providing this resource gives young people an ability to start to rate how strongly they feel about what is happening to them and talk about why they feel as they do.

Sometimes we find that a child consistently overreacts to minor or major events in their lives. Others may underreact. This chart can help kids think through an appropriate way to feel about any given situation.

This chart can be laminated, blown up as a poster, or photocopied for writing directly onto it. Use this chart to help the child rank the events they are dealing with and write notes.

HOW BIG IS MY STRUGGLE?

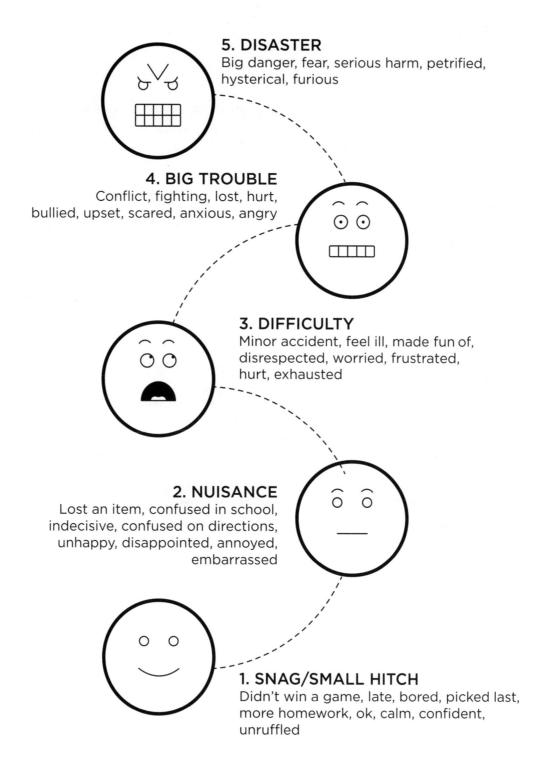

5. DISASTER
Big danger, fear, serious harm, petrified, hysterical, furious

4. BIG TROUBLE
Conflict, fighting, lost, hurt, bullied, upset, scared, anxious, angry

3. DIFFICULTY
Minor accident, feel ill, made fun of, disrespected, worried, frustrated, hurt, exhausted

2. NUISANCE
Lost an item, confused in school, indecisive, confused on directions, unhappy, disappointed, annoyed, embarrassed

1. SNAG/SMALL HITCH
Didn't win a game, late, bored, picked last, more homework, ok, calm, confident, unruffled

What Pushes Your Buttons?

What You Need:

What Pushes Your Buttons? worksheet
Pen or pencil

Goals:

Help young people identify what things create strong reactions in them and why. We want to explore the reactions and emotions that are problematic and consider how to speak to those struggles. This activity works with children ages seven and older.

Directions:

Sit down with the young person and work on the activity together. Begin by asking them to circle all the things on the list that make them feel angry, frustrated, upset, etc. Let them circle as many or few as they'd like. Ask if there are other items not listed they would like you to add. Write those down as well.

Walk through each question following, and prompt them to think about what is going on inside of them. What motivates their frustration or reaction?

Follow-up Questions:

After children have circled all the items that apply to them, ask:

- What are the ones you struggle with most? Put a star next to them.
- What are the ones you struggle with the least? Underline those.
- Do you have a top two or three that are the hardest? What are they?

Things to Observe:

Look for important themes and see what rises to the surface.

- Where do they struggle most?
- Are they ever provoked by family members in unhelpful/unhealthy ways?
- Are they put in situations that bring out the worst in them, and/or where they demand the world around them bends to their will?
- Are they open to change? Do they feel hopeful or discouraged?
- Where do they go for help? Are they humble? Teachable?

WHAT PUSHES YOUR BUTTONS?

- Not getting my way
- My siblings provoking me
- Telling me what to do
- When I think something is unfair
- My mistakes
- Being rejected
- Losing a game
- Doing poorly in school
- Being laughed at
- When I am rushed
- When I am embarrassed
- When I am misunderstood
- Change of plans
- Being judged
- Too much talking
- Too many instructions
- Being interrupted
- Bad news
- Getting hurt

- Work/chores
- Mean people
- Starring at me
- Ignoring me
- Others' mistakes
- Having to work with others
- Getting up in front of classmates
- Hurting my feelings
- Getting in trouble
- Calling on me/attention
- Being told "no"
- Lecturing me
- Touching me
- Too much noise
- Being provoked
- When I am hungry or tired
- Being late
- Homework and tests
- Too much work

When I get upset I:

When I do this, what do others around me say or do?

Does my response help or hurt others? Why?

Does my response help or hurt me? Why?

What do you want to change, or not want to change?

Brainstorm together: What does God have to say?

Brainstorm together: What can we do to work on this?

What Gives Me Anxiety?

What You Need:

What Gives Me Anxiety? worksheet
Pen or pencil

Goals:

This activity is most often used with children or teens who are identifying anxiety as something they struggle with. The activity helps us identify what they get anxious about, how they tend to process the reasons why they are anxious, and then what they do with that information (how they cope).

Directions:

Explain that everyone experiences anxiety in life. Whether the catalyst is imagined or real, big or small, we all battle anxiety in some form. The worksheet includes a list of common things that make people feel nervous or anxious.

Have children circle the items that make them feel anxious. Ask if there is anything that is not on the list that they would like to add. If so, write those items down for them.

Talk through each of the following questions on the worksheet. Encourage them to think about each question and how they can begin addressing their fears and anxieties.

Follow-up Questions:

- Are there anxieties you do not want to let go of?
- Are there temptations you have, or places where you give in to certain anxieties? What does that look like?
- Do others you know have similar fears/anxieties? Who?

Things to Observe:

As with many of these activities, you are looking for patterns and themes. What catches your attention? How do their parent(s) respond to the anxiety? Is it helpful or unhelpful? Where do they see Christ, or their need for him? How receptive are they to change?

WHAT GIVES ME ANXIETY?

Everyone experiences anxiety in life. Whether the catalyst is imagined or real, big or small, we all battle anxiety in some form. Below is a list of common things that make people feel nervous or anxious. Circle the ones that apply to you.

Loud noises	Talking to people	Failure	Anger	Physical harm
Conflict	Big crowds	Heights	Bugs	Bad weather
Being alone	Rejection	The future	The past	Animals
Being around people	Mistakes	Change	School	Family problems
Getting sick	Death	Clowns	Bullying	Not fitting in
The dark	Closed spaces	Flying	Snakes	Eating in front of others
Doctor visits	Needles	Dentist	Ghosts	Public speaking
Scary movies	Blood	Zombies	Being lost	Losing a parent
Money	Fire	Yelling	Bad dreams	Being misunderstood
Criticism	Strong emotions	Spiders	Judgment	Not good enough

Other:

What are your top three fears? Why?

What do you do when you feel anxious about these things?

Do you think your solution works? What doesn't work? Why?

Do you talk to God about your anxieties? Do you think he can help you?

What do you think he has to say about them?

Let's brainstorm together: What does God say in the Bible about these fears?

How can this help you? What are things we can do?

Alien Activity

What You Need:

Alien Activity worksheet

Pen, pencil, colored pencils, or markers

Goals:

Young people often express feeling different or "alien" in comparison to their peers. This might be due to them having a disability, growing up with different family or cultural values, struggles with body image, or any number of other reasons they feel they don't fit in or aren't accepted. When you know this is a struggle for a young person, you can use the following image of an alien to help draw out their perceptions about ways they do and don't fit in.

The goal is to understand their experiences, and then take what you've learned and consider how you will engage with the struggles they uncover. This activity works with children ages seven and older.

Directions:

Tell the young person that you'd like to brainstorm all the ways that he or she feels (or sees himself or herself) as different. Encourage the child to share as many things as he/she can think of. You can write down as many things as the child tells you, or allow the child to write them down (depending on preference). Remember, many kids find it cumbersome to write, so offering to write encourages more sharing.

This could also be used with stickers for younger kids who enjoy them. You can use dots or little alien stickers to place on the picture.

Follow-up Questions:

Once children say they are finished, you can ask these questions:

- What are some ways you feel different or like an alien?
- What are some traits about you that you think others say or believe make you different?
- Are there differences you are proud of? What are they?
- What differences do you wish you could change?
- What differences wouldn't you change, even if others did not accept you?
- What do you think God has to say about you? Why?
- Do you think there could be good in being different? Why or why not?

Things to Observe:

What themes emerge for this child? Do they stem from mistreatment, conflict, internal insecurity, disability, or something else? How do the parents engage with the struggle?

Begin thinking about how you would approach helping the child. How does Scripture speak to their struggles? How do you need to move the child toward different beliefs or thinking? See also the "God Says You Are" sheet (page 157), to help children think this through.

ALIEN ACTIVITY

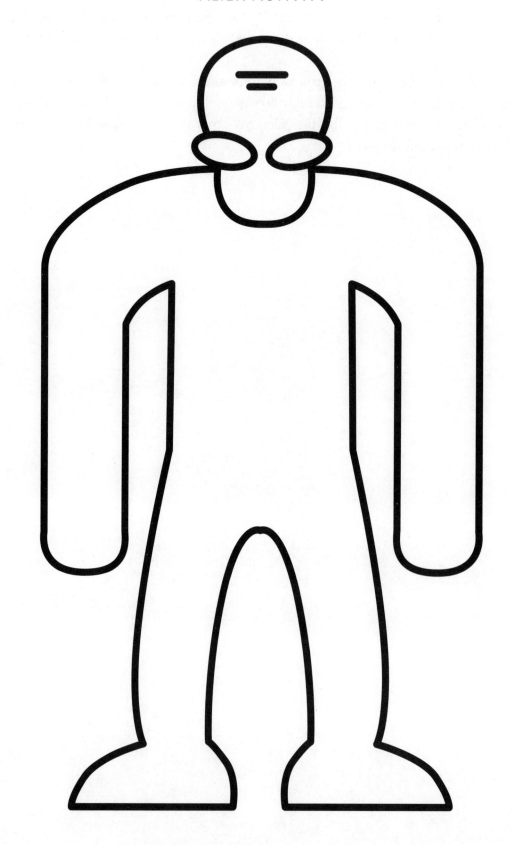

What's under the Surface?

What You Need:

> What's under the Surface? worksheet
> Pen or pencil

Goals:

The goal of this activity is to help young people and/or their parents to identify what worrisome behaviors they are noticing in the child or teen's life, and to start investigating what situations or motives might be underneath the problematic behavior.

For example, a parent may bring a child in for anger issues, but what is going on underneath is actually hurt and anxiety over a family member's death. Perhaps a child comes to counseling struggling with self-injury, only for you to find out they are being bullied or mistreated by a classmate. There are a variety of ways to discuss what you can observe on the outside versus what is going on inside a counselee, or what problem initially brings a family to counseling versus what underlying issues are uncovered in the counseling process.

Brainstorming healthier/godlier actions will be useful for expressing what the child feels underneath as well as finding ways to resolve the underlying struggles and the behaviors above the surface.

Directions:

This is often helpful to do with parents and children. It can be done together to help the family understand that what brings people to counseling may have deeper underlying causes. A child's behavior may be a symptom of disruption in the home, events going on at school, or other outside factors. It may also help parents understand that the negative behavior going on externally is reflective of struggles or beliefs going on internally.

This exercise can be used with a young person to help them think through what they feel, do, or how others perceive them. You will want to adapt this to the needs of the situation.

Following the picture, there are questions to facilitate the discussion. Help the young person to identify the behaviors that are troubling and require help. As you go through the questions together, begin helping them consider what is driving their struggle.

Follow-up Questions:

Follow up questions often flow from what you are uncovering as you talk. You will want to consider if issues arise that require parental involvement, or the help of another outside individual. You'll be looking for issues that arise that may shape the direction or focus of your time with the child.

Things to Observe:

You will take more time with some questions and less with others depending on the child's insight. You may also need to brainstorm ideas to prompt their thinking.

It may also be beneficial to have a parent in the discussion when appropriate. Some young people need help, and having someone they trust and who knows them well may bring insight.

WHAT'S UNDER THE SURFACE?

1. What behaviors do people see in you that concern them?

2. Why do you think they are concerned for you?

3. How do you feel about the reaction you get from others?

4. Why do you think you do the things you do?

5. What would it look like to get help or change?

6. What has helped in the past?

7. What hasn't helped?

8. Are you open to allowing others to help you? Why or why not?

9. Let's brainstorm. What are some things that we can work on together?

10. What are things we can do that would help you with this?

Life at My House

What You Need:

House outline

Coloring and drawing instruments

Goals:

This activity is designed to help kids convey what life is like in their home, and works best with children ages six through twelve. You may come up with many more ideas, depending on what you'd like to know about the child you are working with.

Directions:

Have the child write and draw a picture of each person, and then place the drawing inside the house outline. Some kids like coloring and drawing examples in the house; others like to write their answers; some like to stick stickers of people, animals, and dots next to those they enjoy, fight with, spend time with.

Additional directions you provide will be based upon what information you'd like to gather. See also the Follow-up Questions below.

Follow-up Questions:

Again, the questions you ask will be based upon what information you're looking for.

You may want general information such as:

- Who lives in your house?
- Where do they each live?
- What are the rooms in your house?
- Do you have pets?
- Where is your room? What is it like?

You may want to build understanding of how the family operates:

- What are the rules in your house?
- Who enforces them?
- What are the chores?
- What happens when someone breaks a rule?
- What does your family do together for fun?
- What does a day look like in your house? What does an evening look like at your house?
- What does each person do when he or she is home?

You may want to understand the relationship dynamics in the home:

- Who are you closest to in your family?
- Who aren't you close to?
- Who gets along the best in your house?
- Who do you fight with most, if anyone?
- Who do you spend the most time with?
- Which parent do you spend the most time with?
- Who plays with you?
- Who helps you with your homework?
- Who do you go to when you are sad or upset?
- Who helps you with your feelings?

Things to Observe:

Look for things that might be natural resources and supports for the child (such as a close bond with dad, or the family pet, regular visits with grandma, etc.), or things that could be causing more suffering or struggle for the child (a particular family member, harsh rule, lack of supervision, etc.). Consider also:

- Does the child talk, write, and describe a happy, healthy family environment, or describe conflict and despair?
- What stands out as normal and good? What stands out as concerning or questionable?
- Are there things you understood that you'd like to follow up on? Are there things you are worried about and want to find out more about?

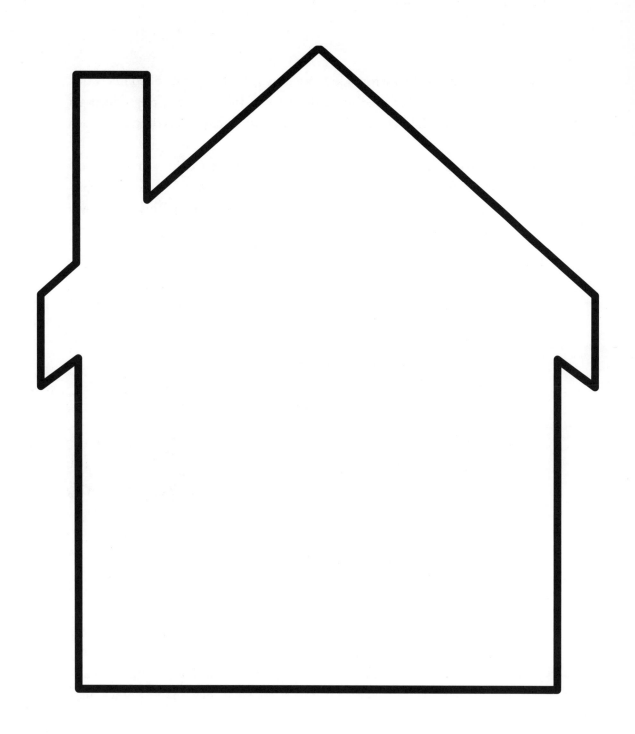

Mom's House, Dad's House

What You Need:

>Two copies of House outline (page 137)
>Pen or pencil

Goals:

When parents divorce, sometimes kids are caught in the middle of conflicts that go on between parents. What used to be the rules in the family all the sudden get turned upside down, or children find they now have two different sets of rules for each home they are visiting.

It is helpful to draw out what the child perceives as differences in each home, how rules change or are inconsistent from home to home, where they feel most comfortable, and why and how they see their relationships with each parent. This activity will work for children ages six and older.

Directions:

Have children label one house "Mom's House" and the other "Dad's House." Ask any or all of the following questions:

- What are the rules in mom's house? What are the rules in dad's house?
- What are the chores in mom's house? dad's house?
- What do you get disciplined for in mom's house? dad's house?
- What are the fun things you do in mom's house? dad's house?
- In whose house does your homework get done?
- What are the differences in each home?
- What are the things that are the same in each house?
- Where do you sleep? What is your room like? Do you share a room with anyone?
- Do you talk about the divorce in mom's house? What do you talk about?
- Do you talk about divorce in dad's house? What do you discuss?
- In what house do you talk most openly/freely?
- In what house do you talk about your feelings?
- What house feels more comfortable? safe? unsafe? stressful? Why?

You can adapt this activity in a variety of ways. Children can write their answers in each house; or you can write it for them, using their words. Some children like to draw pictures of their home life, where people sleep, what they do, etc.; others may use stickers.

Follow-up Questions:

In addition to the questions above, ask as many clarifying questions as needed to better understand what children think, feel, and perceive about each home and why. You can ask if they would give you an example, tell a story, or share an event. This will help you identify places where the child is struggling or the family is in need, and help you discern how to address it.

Things to Observe:

- How healthy or unhealthy is each home the child visits?
- Do the parents attempt to co-parent and share similar rules for the benefit of the children? Are they able to put aside their differences for the sake of the children?
- Does the child feel put in the middle of their parents' differences? Are they forced to appease the emotions or hostility of either parent?
- Are there things you need to help either a child or parent work on?

Brainstorming

What You Need:

> Brainstorming worksheet
> Writing instruments

Goals:

Often young people have a great deal going on inside of them. However, when asked, they freeze, their minds go blank, or they feel overwhelmed with where to start. It can feel like there is a storm going on in their minds. There may be a lot of thoughts swirling around that can cause confusion, anxiety, stress, agitation, or feel overpowering. One way to help is by slowing the storm down and looking at what is going on in their thoughts.

This activity slants toward older kids, but children as young as eight or nine may be astute enough to do this.

Directions:

Ask the child or teen to begin listing all the things they think about. There is no right or wrong; they are simply trying to do a "brain dump"—to take what is going on in their brains and dump as much of it as they can onto the paper. They can write down the thoughts as they come, but if you write what they say they are freed up just to brainstorm and can think more quickly and easily. You/they can write in the mind/brain, the face around it, etc.

Once your brainstorming is done, you can begin sorting out together the cause(s) of their struggles. Ask some of the Follow-up Questions below for clarification.

Follow-up Questions:
- Circle the top three overwhelming thoughts.
- Underline the ones that bother you the least.
- Star the ones you want help with most.
- When do these thoughts tend to overcome you? What is going on at the time?
- What or who helps you when there is a storm going on inside your brain?
- What or who doesn't help?

Things to Observe:

Take what is discussed, and then evaluate some of the themes and key concerns you see for the child or teen. How you begin to address them will depend on what you uncover.

BRAINSTORMING

Chapter 8

Expressive Activities That Speak into Children's Hearts and Challenges

The wise of heart is called discerning, and sweetness of speech increases persuasiveness.

(Proverbs 16:21)

The previous chapter detailed many ways in which we can get to know our counselees well. In this process, we must be slow to jump to conclusions about their problems or heart struggles, and instead demonstrate to them that we hear them and really want to know them (Proverbs 18:2). In order to speak truth wisely to those whom we counsel, we are compelled by the love of Christ to first draw them out and listen well.

Once this foundation of trust has been established and we have been able to help uncover some of the thoughts, troubles, and other struggles our counselees face, part of our essential stewardship as counselors is to speak back into the various situations we bring to light.

Once we have succeeded in drawing out our counselee, our job has only just begun. Our temptation is to simply tell children and teens what they need to fix and pick a verse in the Bible for them to memorize. When shared in a swift or impersonal way, this approach is not rich enough to take the whole person into account, nor does it make the young person in front of us feel heard, loved, and known. Speaking gospel-saturated truth winsomely to our counselee is the goal.

Scripture is not boring, dull, or impersonal—it is rich, deeply personal and meaningful, full of life, and clearly lights the path before us. Hebrews 4:12 tells us, "For the word of God is living and active, sharper than any two-edged sword, piercing to the division of soul and of spirit, of joints and of marrow, and discerning the thoughts and intentions of the heart."

We must strive to show the attractiveness of the gospel. How we speak of the Lord and his ways can either make our counselees want to know him personally or can repel them further away. We must look for ways to talk about struggles, life, the Lord, and Scripture and make the transformative power of the gospel personally relevant to youth on their level. This section will offer just a few suggestions on how we can show the beauty of Christ and his ways.

For example, many young people see the Bible as irrelevant, a killjoy, or unhelpful, particularly concerning dating, sexuality, or sexual identity. This happens often because we talk about relationships and sexuality as if biblical principles are a list of dos and don'ts, rather than a gift from God who wants the best for his children. We need to communicate clearly that God is not anti-sex—he created it and therefore it is good. We need to articulate that it is such a precious gift that it only leads to blessing when it is used the way he intended. The boundaries are there to protect us from destruction.

This concept can be illustrated with a smartphone. You can hold one in front of a teen and brainstorm together all the things it can do (send texts, enable voice or video calls, facilitate social media, play music, etc.). Then you can talk about the limitations of the phone and what it can't do (it can't fly, swim in the ocean, make dinner, or clean my house). Why? Because it wasn't created to do that. I can throw it off a building and demand that it fly, but I shouldn't be surprised when it breaks. Would you and I get angry at the maker of the smartphone if that happened? Do we call up Apple or Samsung or LG and tell them what a killjoy they are for not conforming to our wishes for the phone? We don't because we understand it was only created for certain tasks and if we take it outside its design, it will likely break—it would be our fault.

You can take this illustration to explain that, likewise, God is the creator of sex and sexuality. He made it to work well within a certain context, for our benefit and pleasure. However, anytime we go outside the bounds God created for sex, it will break, it will disappoint, and it will have consequences.

Examples, object lessons, and stories like these can introduce fresh and winsome ways for young people to understand important truths.

Many young people do not believe that God has anything to say about their problems or "modern" issues. It is as though we treat the Bible as irrelevant to life. On the contrary, God's Word offers hope and answers to even the toughest problems we face. Although the way young people struggle feels new and alarming, in many ways their struggles hold nothing new under the sun—there are still themes of acceptance and rejection, lust and greed, selfishness and corruption, mistreatment and suffering, brokenness and conflict. Biblical truth and principles are timeless. We must do the work of connecting our kids back to the Lord and the answers he provides for living godly lives.

Think About It

What You Need:

Think About It and/or Talk It Out worksheets

Goals:

Getting children and teens to slow down and sort through situations is essential to helping them learn to respond well. Walking a young person through the following questions slows down events and situations so that you can discover where things went wrong, and talk through how to think, feel, or respond differently.

It also acts as a mirror to children, helping them see what they were functionally believing or thinking in the midst of a event. We want to reinterpret children's life events in light of truth. We often tend to look at things through a godless lens—one void of God. When we bring God and his ways into the story, it begins to accurately make sense out of their experiences.

Directions:

Use either the Think About It or Talk It Out worksheets provided. Both accomplish the same task but offer different ways to process an experience. These questions can be journaled throughout the week, talked out with a trusted adult, or talked through with you.

Follow-up Questions:

Any follow-up discussion will be based on what flows from processing the questions in the worksheet you use.

Things to Observe:

Seek to understand how young people think and respond, while also helping them understand their own motivations better. Look for faulty beliefs or thinking they are unaware of.

- How are they tempted to respond? Are there patterns?
- What do they need to change?
- Where do they need a clearer picture of who God is and what he has to say to them?

THINK ABOUT IT

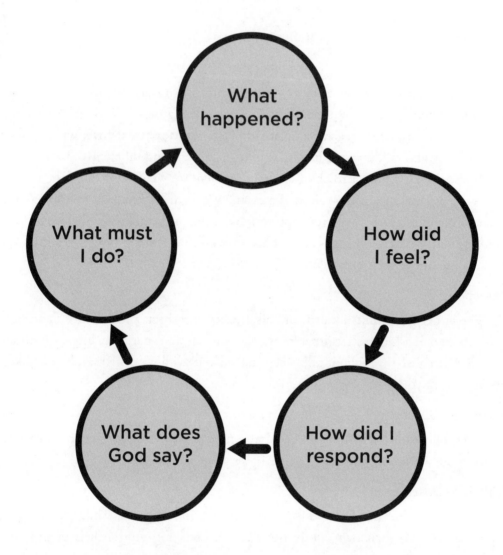

1. What happened? What was the situation?

2. How did I feel about what happened?

3. What did I think about it? Why?

4. What did I do about it? How did I respond?

5. What does God have to say about it? How do I know?

6. How does that help me change the way I think about it?

7. What should I do now? How should I respond?

TALK IT OUT

1 What happened?

2 How did I feel about it?

3 What did I think about it?

4 What did I do about it? How did I respond?

5 What does God say about it?

6 How does that change how I should think about it?

7 How do I need to respond to it now?

My Problem Says/God Says

What You Need:

My Problem Says/God Says worksheet

Goals:

This simple worksheet can help facilitate discussion about what a young person believes versus what God has to say about his or her problem.

Directions:

Have the child write the identified problem/struggle on the top of the page. Brainstorm with the child all the things he or she believes to be true about the problem (it will never change, it will never get better, it's too hard, etc.).

Next, work on a list of truths of what God says about their problem/struggle (God works in us, this is temporary, God gives us what we need). Look up verses, passages, and stories/examples in Scripture that demonstrate this and talk out how it applies to his or her life.

Follow-up Questions:

Work at helping children make meaningful connections:

- Why do you think it is hard to believe what God has to say?
- What would it look like to believe this truth?
- How would it change what you do or how you live each day?
- How would you put each truth into practice?

Things to Observe:

We want truth to transform and renew children's hearts and minds. What are the things they really need to hear and believe?

Look for ways you might reiterate these truths throughout your meeting. Are there compelling stories or testimonies you can share? There may be songs, quotes, or specific stories from Scripture that this young person can map onto his or her personal struggle.

MY PROBLEM SAYS/GOD SAYS

The problem I have is:

My problem says:	God says:
I can't figure it out.	I will show you the way to go (Psalm 32:8).
It will be turn out bad.	I will work everything for good (Romans 8:28).
I'm not able.	I am able (2 Corinthians 9:8).
It's impossible.	All things are possible (Luke 18:27).
I can't do it.	You can do all things with my help (Philippians 4:13).
I can't keep trying.	I will give you grace (2 Corinthians 12:9).
I can't handle it.	I will supply everything you need (Philippians 4:19).
I'm all alone.	I will never leave you (Hebrews 13:5).
I'm not smart.	I will give you wisdom (1 Corinthians 1:30).
I'm afraid.	I am your strength and defense (Isaiah 12:2).
I'm too weak.	In your weakness, I am strong (2 Corinthians 12:9).
No one cares.	I love you with a never-ending love (Jeremiah 31:3).

What can I do now?

The Fruit Tree

What You Need:

Fruit Tree image
Stickers of fruit
Pens and/or colored pens

Goals:

Real change cannot happen apart from a transformation in what rules us. When we desire to live life God's way, the fruit in our lives demonstrates this. It is marked by honesty, integrity, good choices, kind words, and trust. The fruit points to what is going on underneath the surface, and what informs and feeds our souls will define what comes forth from us.

As we talk to children and teens about their desires and behaviors, we want to help them understand what is informing their choices and behaviors—and how they can transform those thoughts, choices, and behaviors.

Kids and teens are seldom self-aware of what drives their behavior, and sometimes can't even see how behavior brings on good or bad consequences. We want to help build an understanding *of them* and an understanding *for them*. We pursue knowing them well, and then help them know and understand themselves.

Young people can often identify the behaviors that got them in trouble or brought them to counseling. Whether it is self-injury, depression, anger, divorce, or social difficulties, we can work with identifying the fruit in their lives and strive to make the connections to what is going on at the level of their heart. The Fruit Tree image can be used to bridge the gap between children's choices, behaviors, and actions (the fruit), and what informs their decisions, motivates them, dominates their heart (the roots).

The more we seek to have hearts filled with a love for God and his ways, the less room we have to live for ourselves—and vice versa. The more we see our motivations, the more we can ask the Lord to change them. Some fruit may change, some may stay the same, but the motives for our actions become pure and right.

Directions:

Before your meeting, take the Fruit Tree image and turn it into any poster size. You will want to laminate it; this way you will be able to use dry erase markers and use it in many contexts, from child to child, to group or youth group settings, to Sunday school or working with your own children at home. You can draw and write all over it, then simply wipe it down when you are done.

You will also want to cut out various types of fruit (or only one type, if you wish) and laminate those; try to make them big enough that you can write on them. Then, add VELCRO® strips onto the tree and ground, and onto the back sides of the fruit, so you are able to stick the fruit on the tree, take it off and move it to the ground, or move it around the tree.

With the child, talk through Luke 6:43–45: "For no good tree bears bad fruit, nor again does a bad tree bear good fruit, for each tree is known by its own fruit. For figs are not gathered from thornbushes, nor are grapes picked from a bramble bush. The good person out of the good treasure of his heart produces good, and the evil person out of his evil treasure produces evil, for out of the abundance of the heart his mouth speaks."

Explain how the passage compares us to a tree; our actions and choices are our fruit. Ask children what they believe to be their fruit in their lives (good and bad). Let them put a fruit sticker on the tree and tell you what it represents; write down what they say next to it. Have them brainstorm as many as they can think of. If they have not brought it up, talk about what fruit/behavior has created trouble for them.

What can sometimes be difficult for young people is that there is often good fruit and bad fruit mixed together. Take one sticker at a time and try talking through what that behavior says about what is motivating them. Are they living life "God's Way" or "My Way"? Do they behave that way because they desire to please the Lord, or because it serves them in some way?

It is helpful for a young person to see that sometimes we are divided in our desires. Sometimes we make wise godly choices, and other times we are driven by our own wants. It is also helpful to discuss how sometimes a fruit can look good but is really driven by selfish purposes. For example, a child may do something nice for his or her sibling, but with the goal of getting one of their toys. Or a teen may strive for good grades, but it is out of a desire to look good in front of their peers, or fear of failure. To help illustrate these things:

- You can draw arrows from the bad fruit to the ground, or the heart that lives life "My Way."
- You can place stickers on the ground, representing the rotten fruit.
- You can write, on the roots, the things you identify as motivating behavior.

Follow-up Questions:

This activity is also a helpful way to introduce how the Lord transforms us to be more like him and how to expect Christ to work when we allow him be Lord of our lives. It may be helpful to demonstrate that when we allow the Lord to direct our desires, the bad/rotten fruit falls off the tree to the ground, and good fruit begins to grow. Ask:

- What things do you need to change (or would like to work on)?
- What would change look like for you?
- How can I help you in making that change?

Things to Observe:

How do children make sense of their behavior and motives? How do you need to make the connections clear for them? We do not want to simply emphasize behavior change, but go deeper and consider how their lives can be motivated by love for the Lord and his ways. He is the source of all real hope and change.

The following passages talk about the tree or fruit imagery and may be beneficial, depending on the discussion:

> Psalm 1:3: "He is like a tree planted by streams of water that yields its fruit in its season, and its leaf does not wither. In all that he does, he prospers."

> Proverbs 11:30: "The fruit of the righteous is a tree of life, and whoever captures souls is wise."

> Proverbs 13:12: "Hope deferred makes the heart sick, but desire fulfilled is a tree of life."

> Proverbs 15:4 (NIV): "The soothing tongue is a tree of life, but a perverse tongue crushes the spirit."

> Ezekiel 47:12: "And on the banks, on both sides of the river, there will grow all kinds of trees for food. Their leaves will not wither, nor their fruit fail, but they will bear fresh fruit every month, because the water for them flows from the sanctuary. Their fruit will be for food, and their leaves for healing."

> John 15:1–4: "I am the true vine, and my Father is the vinedresser. Every branch in me that does not bear fruit he takes away, and every branch that does bear fruit he prunes, that it may bear more fruit. Already you are clean because of the word that I have spoken to you. Abide in me, and I in you. As the branch cannot bear fruit by itself, unless it abides in the vine, neither can you, unless you abide in me."

Scripture is rich with imagery that makes connections from us to the tree/branches/vine. In addition to the above passages, Judges 9:8–15 offers an allegory of the thornbush; Luke 13:6–9 provides the imagery of the fig tree and the call to Israel; Paul illustrates us being grafted into the tree in Romans 11; and Revelation 22:2 and 19 (as well as Ezekiel 47:7 and 12) describe the Tree of Life. So be wise, as you faithfully apply the Word of God to the need of the moment.

Mirror Activity

Things you need:

> God Says . . . handout
> Small handheld mirror or a copy of the mirror worksheet (page 159)
> Pen or pencil

Goals:

Children and teens are often tempted to find identity in what others (or the culture) defines as valuable. There are many voices and images that bombard young people and threaten to shape their self-image: secular values and images, concepts of love and sexuality, romance, success, and normalcy. This activity is helpful with most older elementary kids and teens, especially those with body-image struggles, issues of peer pressure, or disabilities that they feel define them as different or "less than."

Directions:

Set up your "mirror" (whether handheld or paper), and ask young people to talk through (or list) what they see or believe about themselves when they look in the mirror. Allow them to take their time to write down their thoughts or offer to do so for them. Get them to brainstorm all the ideas they can come up with. Some will answer your question based on how they see themselves; others will answer based on what they believe or have heard others think about them.

Follow-up Questions:

Once you're done, consider what they have shared and how to incorporate the following talking points:

- What are the things you do to try to measure up or fit in with others?
- Is there anything wrong with the things you do?
- Is there anything good or beneficial about the things you do (e.g., exercise, buy nice clothes, build an online image)?

Next, talk about how sometimes the issue is not the behavior itself, but *the degree to which we allow those activities to dictate our worth.*

- Does it shape the way you feel about yourself today?
- Does it inform how you believe others see you?
- Does it alter your actions?
- Does it drive your behavior?
- How do your habits reflect your functional beliefs (i.e., what your actions reveal about what you really believe)?

Things to Observe:

We want to help young people see that the images they create for themselves—the people they see in the mirror—harm themselves and prevent genuine relationships for several reasons:

- We can only see others through the lens in which they see us.
- It enslaves us to an image or what others think of our image.
- It prevents us from being known or knowing others.
- It destroys relationship—it separates "us" from "them."
- We become obsessed with self, with no room for concern about others.

Take out the God Says . . . handout, and ask the young person to think about what it would be like to put down or destroy the mirrors they are holding, and instead choose to believe what the Bible reflects about who they are.

All true beauty and success stems from God's standard of these things. He is not anti-beauty; he is the creator of it. However, beauty or success is not meant to give us our value or worth—that can only come from him. The Bible acknowledges that great and small exists in every exchange of life. There are the attractive and unattractive, the famous and those who live quiet lives, the successful and unsuccessful, the smart and those with little intelligence. How quickly a God-ordained difference becomes a tool we use to measure ourselves.

The answer is not to focus more on ourselves but less, and to make the Lord and his will our proper focus. Are we teaching our teens to find identity, comfort, and safety in human relationships, or in Christ? We want children to learn to find identity and hope in the One who will not fail, disappoint, or reject them. Any agenda for change must focus on the thoughts and desires of the heart.

GOD SAYS . . .

God says you are fearfully and wonderfully made.
I praise you because I am fearfully and wonderfully made; your works are wonderful, I know that full well. (Psalm 139:14, NIV)

God says you will always be loved.
And I am convinced that nothing can ever separate us from God's love. Neither death nor life, neither angels nor demons, neither our fears for today nor our worries about tomorrow—not even the powers of hell can separate us from God's love. No power in the sky above or in the earth below—indeed, nothing in all creation will ever be able to separate us from the love of God that is revealed in Christ Jesus our Lord. (Romans 8:38–39, NLT)

God says you belong.
God decided in advance to adopt us into his own family by bringing us to himself through Jesus Christ. This is what he wanted to do, and it gave him great pleasure. (Ephesians 1:5, NLT)

God says he will give you power, love, and a sound mind.
For God gave us a spirit not of fear but of power and love and self-control. (2 Timothy 1:7)

God says he gave his son for you.
For God so loved the world, that he gave his only Son, that whoever believes in him should not perish but have eternal life. (John 3:16)

God says he can heal you.
But he was pierced for our transgressions, he was crushed for our iniquities; the punishment that brought us peace was on him, and by his wounds we are healed. (Isaiah 53:5, NIV)

God says he is your strength.
God arms me with strength, and he makes my way perfect. (Psalm 18:32, NLT)

God says he will make you complete.
So you also are complete through your union with Christ, who is the head over every ruler and authority. (Colossians 2:10, NLT)

God says you are his.
Do not fear, for I have redeemed you; I have summoned you by name; you are mine. (Isaiah 43:1, NIV)

God says you are forgiven.

I am writing to you who are God's children because your sins have been forgiven through Jesus. (1 John 2:12, NLT)

God says he will always be with you.

Do not be afraid; do not be discouraged, for the LORD your God will be with you wherever you go. (Joshua 1:9, NIV)

God says he has plans for you.

For I know the plans I have for you, declares the LORD, plans for welfare and not for evil, to give you a future and a hope. (Jeremiah 29:11)

God says you have value and purpose.

And who knows whether you have not come . . . for such a time as this? (Esther 4:14)

God says he will lead you.

Whether you turn to the right or to the left, your ears will hear a voice behind you, saying "This is the way; walk in it." (Isaiah 30:21, NIV)

God says he will give you peace and comfort.

Peace I leave with you; my peace I give to you. Not as the world gives do I give to you. Let not your hearts be troubled, neither let them be afraid. (John 14:27)

God says he can give you joy.

I have told you these things so that you will be filled with my joy. Yes, your joy will overflow! (John 15:11, NLT)

MIRROR WORKSHEET

Anxiety Activity

What You Need:

Anxiety Activity worksheet

Goals:

The idea of this activity is to take Philippians 4:6–9 and apply it to a young person's struggles. We want to help make Scripture relevant to the child's personal life. This can be adapted for most ages, but will work best with kids and teens who possess the ability to think through these questions with you.

Directions:

Walk through the Anxiety Activity worksheet with the young person. Take time to slow down and explore each statement and question. Talk through what each term means, and the ways it changes our perspective.

Follow-up Questions:

- What does this passage remind us to say, do, or think?
- Does it encourage you or discourage you? Why?
- What are steps you can take to put this into practice?

Things to Observe:

- Where is the child struggling to make meaningful connections to his or her experience? How can you help bridge the gap for him or her?
- Does the conversation lead you to other passages or verses that are helpful or applicable to the discussion? If so, talk through those passages, drawing out similar questions and action steps.

ANXIETY ACTIVITY

Do not be anxious about anything, but in everything by prayer and supplication with thanksgiving let your requests be made known to God. And the peace of God, which surpasses all understanding, will guard your hearts and your minds in Christ Jesus.

Finally, brothers, whatever is true, whatever is honorable, whatever is just, whatever is pure, whatever is lovely, whatever is commendable, if there is any excellence, if there is anything worthy of praise, think about these things. What you have learned and received and heard and seen in me—practice these things, and the God of peace will be with you. (Philippians 4:6–9)

What things make you anxious or afraid?

When this happens, what would it look like to "let your requests be made known to God"? How do you give them to God in prayer?

What do you think thanksgiving has do with praying and our anxieties? What are the things you can be thankful for?

What do you think the peace of God is, and how would that look in your situation?

After we give our anxiety over to the Lord, what do we do next? Philippians tells us to control or direct the way we think, in the verses 8–9: "Finally, brothers, whatever is true, whatever is honorable, whatever is just, whatever is pure, whatever is lovely, whatever is commendable, if there is any excellence, if there is anything worthy of praise, think about these things. What you have learned and received and heard and seen in me—practice these things, and the God of peace will be with you."

Let's talk through what each term means and ways you can think about these things. Let's brainstorm things you can think, say, or do that reflect each of these categories.

Whatever is true (what is right, good, and accurate)

Whatever is honorable (moral, righteous, noble, respectable)

Whatever is just (impartial, right, wise, good to all)

Whatever is pure (wholesome, untainted, uncorrupted, virtuous)

Whatever is lovely (attractive, pleasant, good, easy to delight in before God)

Whatever is commendable (admirable, estimable, venerable)

If there is any excellence or worthy of praise (worthy of being in awe of, amazed by)

Think about these things. How do you choose to think about or dwell upon these things? What will that do for you?

What you have learned and received and heard and seen in me—practice these things. . . How can you practice these things at home, school, and other places?

. . . and the peace of God will be with you. What do you think that will look like in your life? How will that change/help you?

Who Is King?

What You Need:

Kingship Passages handout

Throne and/or crown handouts

King's robe and crown (if role-playing with younger children)

Goals:

In too many homes, children are being raised to believe they are there to be served and catered to. In other homes the opposite exists—home life, routines, and people are expected to revolve around the agenda of one or both parents. Both paradigms are equally faulty.

There is only one King: the Lord Jesus Christ. Every home and every individual is to live in submission to the King. It's not that our will be done, but that his will be done. Parents are not rulers, and children are not their subjects. They are stewards of the King; parents are given the responsibility to steward and shepherd their children, family, and resources for the glory of the King, not their own benefit. Likewise, children and teens need to be raised to know that they do not sit on the throne; they must remember who their King is and allow that to shape life and behavior.

Talking to kids about what it means to step off the throne and let Jesus be King can benefit in several ways:

- Young people are shown that the world does not revolve around them.
- We teach godly submission and humility; this can also foster great conversation about what it should look like.
- We cultivate a servant's heart in children, rather than a mini-god mindset.
- We offer comfort and security in believing a mighty King cares for his people. This can provide relief for those who fear letting go of control.
- We instill belief that whatever the King does or allows can be trusted and will be for our good.

Directions:

Personalize this activity according to what the child, teen, or family is struggling with. What ways do they struggle to let Jesus be King in their lives? In what ways do they attempt to sit on the throne or wear the crown? Who do they do this with? What does it look like in their lives?

For younger children: You could have the child role-play as a king, putting on a robe or crown and carrying a scepter. You can ask them:

- If you were king, what would your rules be?
- How would you maintain peace? prevent conflict? rule justly? deal with disobedience?

Look for ways to demonstrate how impossible it is for us to be king and all the difficulties we must try to navigate. Make connections to how much better it would be to be a subject of a king who is wise, just, loving, and good rather than to try to do his job.

For teens (or younger children): Use the handout of the throne or crown, and have the child talk out these questions:

- If you could be king in your home, school, circumstances, what would you do?
- How would you deal with the difficult people, your parents or siblings, or peers?
- What would you change?
- What if others did not listen or follow your rules?
- What would be your limitations?

You can have the child write out what he or she thinks he or she would do, or you could list out the ways you see him or her trying to be king. The goal is to help children see how they are their own mini-gods and how they bring their own ruin.

Follow-up Questions:

Based on the need, below are some suggested approaches to further discussion.

- Have children list the ways they can step off the throne and grow to trust the Lord, or ways he can reveal his kingship in their lives and be trusted.
- Talk through (or list) the ways the Lord is all knowing, all powerful, is everywhere, and can handle everything.
- Go through the Kingship Passages handout together, then ask if they think they could do a better job than the Lord. Many times we do think we can do a better job, so be prepared to talk about the ways we fall short in that role.

Things to Observe:

How are children engaging with the topic? Take time to paint a vivid picture of what a good, benevolent King we serve and why. Talk about his character, how he deals with us as children, and his desire to woo us and not ruin us.

KINGSHIP PASSAGES

1 Chronicles 29:11–12

Yours, O LORD, is the greatness and the power and the glory and the victory and the majesty, for all that is in the heavens and in the earth is yours. Yours is the kingdom, O LORD, and you are exalted as head above all. Both riches and honor come from you, and you rule over all. In your hand are power and might, and in your hand it is to make great and to give strength to all.

Psalm 103:19

The LORD has established his throne in the heavens, and his kingdom rules over all.

Isaiah 37:16

O LORD of hosts, the God of Israel, enthroned above the cherubim, you are the God, you alone, of all the kingdoms of the earth; you have made heaven and earth.

1 Samuel 12:12

And when you saw that Nahash the king of the Ammonites came against you, you said to me, "No, but a king shall reign over us," when the LORD your God was your king.

Psalm 95:3

For the LORD is a great God, and a great King above all gods.

Isaiah 44:6

Thus says the LORD, the King of Israel and his Redeemer, the LORD of hosts: "I am the first and I am the last, besides me there is no god."

1 Timothy 1:17 (NIV)

Now to the King eternal, immortal, invisible, the only God, be honor and glory forever and ever. Amen.

Revelation 15:3

And they sing the song of Moses, the servant of God, and the song of the Lamb, saying, "Great and amazing are your deeds, O Lord God the Almighty! Just and true are your ways, O King of the nations!

Psalm 93:1

> The LORD reigns; he is robed in majesty;
>   the LORD is robed; he has put on strength as his belt.
> Yes, the world is established; it shall never be moved.

Psalm 145:11–13

> They shall speak of the glory of your kingdom and tell of your power, to make known to the children of man your mighty deeds, and the glorious splendor of your kingdom. Your kingdom is an everlasting kingdom, and your dominion endures throughout all generations.

Revelation 19:16

> And on his robe and on his thigh he has a name written, King of kings and Lord of lords.

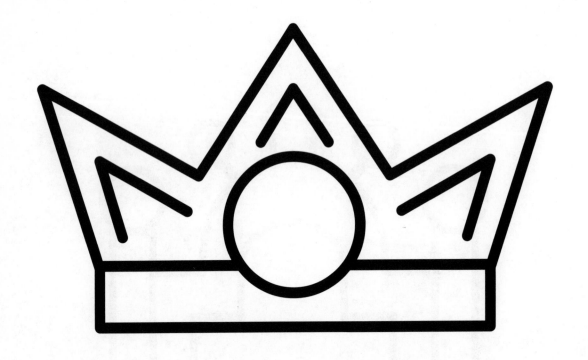

Emotions Highway

What You Need:

Emotions Highway handout

Miniatures of people, roadblocks or fences, traffic signs, cars (enough for each child you're working with), and various emergency vehicles (police, ambulance, helicopter)

Dry-erase markers (optional)

Goals:

Kids often struggle with strong emotions such as anxiety, anger, fear, frustration. At times, the struggle is impulse control, blurting out or reactive behaviors.

The Emotions Highway is a creative way to talk about emotions that feel out of control to children; it also helps kids understand the dynamics and effects of their strong emotions. It gives them a metaphor that they can relate to, so that they can begin incorporating ways they can slow themselves down, as well as slow their emotions down. It also provides a creative way of talking through how mom, dad or any adult can help offer warning signs, guardrails, speed bumps, or pit stops to protect children from getting out of control. This activity works best with children ages five through thirteen.

Directions:

The Emotions Highway handout works best when enlarged to poster size and laminated, so it can be used regularly with miniature things placed on it, or written on with dry-erase markers.

Pull out the handout/poster and begin to talk to kids about their knowledge of highway rules and speeding. Most will love sharing what they know—or telling you when their parents, or others, have broken the rules. Talk about what happens when people speed, who they put at risk, and what the consequences might be. Talk about what "road rage" is. Share how emotions that race out of control can be much like a vehicle racing out of control on a highway.

Next, let children pick vehicles to represent themselves. Have a variety of vehicles to choose from: trucks, motorcycles, race cars, etc. Have them pick vehicles to represent people in their family, school, or life circumstances, and place them on the poster.

Ask what happens when a vehicle speeds down a highway. It is out of control, can't slow down, or make sudden turns or stops. The faster you go, the less likely you are prepared for sudden stops, turns, or roadblocks. It also interferes with your ability to enjoy the ride and to stay within the lines of the road or guardrails. Also ask:

- What are the ways you put others at risk when emotions race too fast?
- What are the consequences?

Next, point out the police cars, which represent the people or ways by which consequences happen. Maybe you'll just get a warning, maybe you'll get a ticket or consequence. Perhaps you've ignored all the warning signs and created such disarray that the consequences are far greater. Ask children, "Who tend to be the police in your life?" (parents, teachers, leaders, coaches, etc.).

Follow-up Questions:
- What's fueling your engine, when you find yourself driving too fast or too recklessly?
- What temptation traps are you vulnerable to (I'm a victim; you made me speed up; I can't slow down; others were speeding so I had to)?
- How could even positive emotions create similar problems? What can you do when you get too excited, even about a good thing?
- What are ways we can help you slow down? How can speed bumps or pit stops help you?
- Where can you pull over to calm down and deal with your emotions (education station, pit stop)?
- What type of pit stops might help you at home (sitting in a comfy chair, going to your room to chill out, swinging on a swing in your yard until you're calm)?
- What signs could a grown-up give you that you're going too fast?

Remind children that pit stops are different from consequences, which only come after they've chosen to ignore all the signs. When the police pull you over, it means you've ignored all the signs given to slow down. Consequences, small or large, will then follow based on the offense.

Things to Observe:

There are practical ways to help kids and parents slow emotions down, while also helping kids to understand what motivates them (anger, control, fear, etc.). Invite a parent to participate in brainstorming ways they can help their kids work on this and language they can adapt to signal the kid needs breaks or help. You want parents or other adults to be able to use the language of racing, speed bumps, and pit stops so kids can resonate with them in a fresh way.

EMOTIONS HIGHWAY

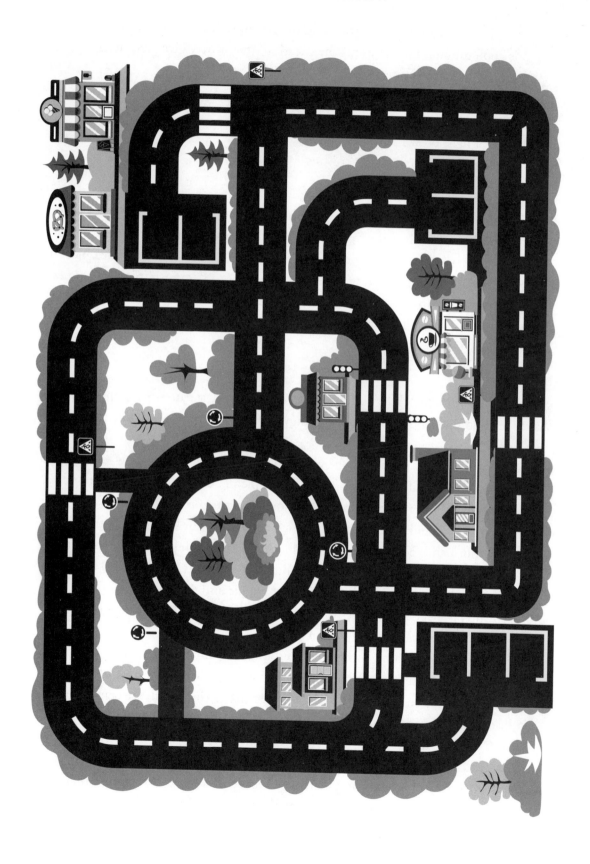

Building Up or Tearing Down

> Let no corrupting talk come out of your mouths, but only such as
> is good for building up, as fits the occasion, that it may give grace to
> those who hear. (Ephesians 4:29)

What You Need:

White or light brown paper lunch bags
Coloring pencils, markers, or crayons

Goals:

The old cliché, "Sticks and stones may break my bones but words will never hurt me," sounds nice, but the reality is that words cut deeply. The purpose of this activity is to help illustrate the impact words have on others. Whether a child is the object of bullying or is the one mistreating others, it is helpful to demonstrate what happens when we tear a person down with words (or behavior). This activity is a great illustration to children of the impact of words, attitudes, and actions, and works best with children ages three through twelve.

Directions:

Sit down with the child and describe how to make a paper-bag puppet. Then, have the child make his or her puppet; you will also make a puppet while the child is working.

When you're both done, tell the child you'd like to talk about how words (and actions) can either build someone up or tear someone down. Put on your puppets, then ask the child to say something unkind or mean to your puppet (such as "You're ugly" or "You're stupid"). After the child says the mean words, slightly crumple the puppet in your hand. Tell the child to say another unkind thing; continue to crumple your puppet with each unkind thing said, until the puppet is in a wrinkled ball.

Talk about how words and actions impact people and tear each other down. The crumpled-up puppet demonstrates the impact words have. We can't always see it from the outside, but they can crush a person's spirit.

Next, ask the child to say something kind to the crumpled-up puppet. Each time a kind word is spoken, uncrumple the puppet little by little, as words of grace are spoken to it. Ask the child what he or she is observing as kind words are being spoken, then discuss the ways we can build someone up/give grace to others by the way we speak.

Place your wrinkled puppet next to the child's puppet, which should still look nice and smooth. Talk about the differences between the two. The puppet that was once rumpled was slowly evened out (though it still has lines and creases) by kind words. However, the impact (the creases) is still evident. The marks have been left and do not go away quickly. Discuss ways you have seen this happen in their lives or the lives of others.

Follow-up Questions:

If the child is one impacted by unkind words, talk about the ways they have been mistreated and in what ways they identify with the puppet. Talk about how God defines who they are; speak words to them that build up and tell them what is true, right, and good.

If the child is someone who bullies others or speaks in unkind ways to others, discuss what Ephesians 4:29 means. Explore what's going on inside of them:

- What are the ways you tear down others through words, actions, even attitudes?
- How do you do this to parents, siblings, or peers?
- What's behind your actions? What motivates you to act like this?
- Do you understand or care about the impact your words, actions, or attitudes are having? Why or why not?
- Brainstorm ways the child could change, and speak words of life or grace to others. What makes that possible? What makes it difficult?

Things to Observe:

Through this discussion, you may unearth other things going on in the child's life. Some kids act out because they have been mistreated or bullied. Some do so due to hurt and brokenness in their family, or because it has been modeled to them. Wisdom considers how to approach the child based on the struggle and need. How does Scripture speak to the issue, and what are winsome ways to communicate this to them?

Taking Thoughts Captive

What You Need:

Taking Thoughts Captive worksheet
Pens, colored pencils, and/or other writing utensils
Stickers (or drawings) of flies

Goals:

There are young people who find it particularly difficult to handle their thoughts. Some struggle with anxious thoughts that bombard them. Some kids may feel overcome by obtrusive or disturbing thoughts, while others may have racing thoughts and ideas they feel they cannot control.

Often the thoughts that bombard them say something about what has consumed them. Is it something they fear? Something they desire? Something that gives them stress? Helping young people understand what exactly is behind the thoughts is important. Another challenge is convincing children that despite *how* the thoughts come, they can control what they do with them.

We need to help children know what to do with their thoughts. Kids need to know that they control their thoughts; their thoughts do not have to control them. One passage that often comes to mind is 2 Corinthians 10:5 (NIV): "We demolish arguments and every pretension that sets itself up against the knowledge of God, and we take captive every thought to make it obedient to Christ."

A picture that most kids can resonate with is one of flies flying around your head. One fly may be annoying, two flies frustrating, but three, four, five flies are downright overwhelming! The more flies, the more distracted, anxious, or stressed we are. We swat one way, and it returns a minute later. We try swatting several away, and it can feel like they are multiplying; we don't know which one to go after first.

Our thoughts can feel like that as well. One upsetting thought may be hard, two may be annoying, but once three or four come, the more burdened and distracted we feel. We don't know how to deal with one thought without another being right there, and before you know it, the first one is back again.

What we want to emphasize is that no matter how and why the thoughts come, we must make a choice what to do with them. Giving kids the awareness that they can choose what to do with their thoughts will also give them the confidence to take action against them and change.

Directions:

Before meeting with the child, make a copy of the Taking Thoughts Captive worksheet. This can also be a poster you blow up, laminate, and use VELCRO® strips on flies that you can take on and off and move around. There are stickers of flies you can purchase; kids love sticking the stickers while you write down what thought that fly represents. You can also draw or use a graphic of the fly, or simply list the thoughts around the head. Look for ways to make this activity more engaging.

With the young person, brainstorm all the thoughts that overwhelm him or her, writing those thoughts down as the child relates them. After you've listed them all out, look for themes or patterns you see and consider ways you can begin addressing what's behind the thoughts.

Remind the child that 2 Corinthians 10:5 says, "we take captive every thought to make it obedient to Christ." Much like flies that will not leave you alone, your thoughts sometimes feel like they attack you and will not go away. When that happens, we want to think, *What does it look like to take each thought captive—or to capture each thought—and make it obedient to the Lord?* We want to capture each thought one by one and decide what to do with it, so it does not keep returning. The only way we can do that is to take our thoughts and make them submit to what God says is true.

Follow-up Questions:

Take one "fly," or thought, at a time, and ask the child:

- What would it look like if you captured that fly and got rid of it?
- How would it feel?
- What does God's Word say about this thought?

Record the answers to the last question on the child's worksheet, so the child can refer back to it later.

Things to Observe:

We do not want to be simplistic or dismissive as we work through this activity. It is important to discern why the child is consumed by each thought you are dealing with, to help them know what is true, and to talk about how they can manage or get rid of that thought.

TAKING THOUGHTS CAPTIVE

My thought says:

God says:

Thought 2 says:

God says:

Thought 3 says:

God says:

Seeking God

What You Need:

Seeking God worksheets

Bible (optional)

Goals:

Psalm 27 talks about what to do when we fear bad things happening. It is a cry for God's protection, as well as a declaration of who God is: he can be trusted and is good. It gives us insight into where our help comes from—not in our circumstances, nor in security that hard things will not happen, but in God's presence in the midst of hard things. Being close to the Lord and knowing he is right there with us is vital in shaping our responses and in reminding us where our hope/comfort is found.

Directions:

Use the worksheet and passage to explain how the young person can seek God in the midst of a difficult situation. Psalm 27:4 (NIV, emphasis added) holds the key to helping us face the "what ifs":

> "One thing I ask from the Lord, this only do I seek: that I may *dwell* in the house of the Lord all the days of my life, to *gaze* on the beauty of the Lord and to *seek* him in his temple."

Each emphasized word is different, but holds a similar truth: it is about God's presence. We want him to be at our right hand, to be our guide, to be our shelter, to give us comfort. A simpler way to put it for elementary-age kids (expressed on the second worksheet) might be the following:

Dig—I want to know what is true and believe what God says.

Dwell—I want Jesus to be my best friend and companion, who is always with me.

Delight—I want to enjoy and take pleasure in being with Jesus.

Discuss each word and work through the questions on the worksheet with the child.

Follow-up Questions:

You can also read through the entire psalm with the child to find helpful ways to summarize what is happening. Ask the young person to brainstorm ways this verse applies to him or her directly, and/or to the situation he or she is currently working through. You can write on the sheet, make a list, or have the child journal through the course of a week.

Things to Observe:

Remember, you are building bridges from Scripture to the child's circumstances and back again. You can build and add onto this depending on what is relevant to the child's life, adding other Bible passages that might speak to the child's situation. How can you encourage the child to see God in his or her day-to-day experiences?

The book *My Heart, Christ's Home Retold for Children*, by Robert Boyd Munger (IVP Books, 2010), can also help young people understand and process these truths.

One thing I ask from the LORD, this only do I seek: that I may dwell in the house of the LORD all the days of my life, to gaze on the beauty of the LORD and to seek him in his temple. (Psalm 27:4, NIV)

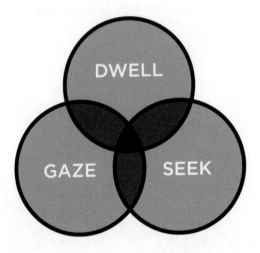

Dwell: *to reside, inhabit, abide in*
What would it look like for you to dwell or reside with the Lord in the midst of this situation?

Gaze: *to regard, contemplate, remain focused or meditate on*
What would it mean to regard, be in awe of, and remain focused on the Lord despite what you're going through?

Seek: *to pursue, strive for, go after*
How could you have a heart that strives after the Lord, rather than fear what might come next?

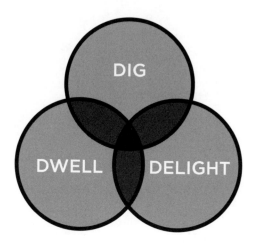

Dig: What does God and his Word have to say about what's going on in my life?

Dwell: What does it look like to draw near to Jesus and invite him to be my best friend?

Delight: How can I enjoy Jesus more and more?

Conclusion

Unleashing Your Own Creativity

My hope is that this book has given you just a taste of the abundant options that are possible when we think well about ministering to young people. God is a God of creativity, and he has given us imaginations that can seek out unique inroads into the hearts of those we reach out to. Each one of our gifts as counselors can be used in a variety of ways as we follow God's call to love people wisely and personally—just as Christ loves us.

God has given each member of the body of Christ different gifts of the Spirit (1 Corinthians 12). Consider your giftings and how they might be used to connect with a hurting or reluctant young person. Perhaps you are strong in compassion and mercy. Maybe you are really gifted at creating stories, or listening might be your strength.

In addition to your more natural skill sets, be a perpetual learner and find out where you can intentionally seek to grow. There are many good books and resources available on storytelling, object lessons, counseling resources, etc. Also learn to rely on others' creativity; watch and learn from them and how they approach helping youth. We all to some degree build off the work others have begun.

CCEF's late director David Powlison, a wise and gifted thinker, often generously allowed others to utilize or build on his ideas, saying "It's OK; I got them all from Scripture." We always want to give credit where credit is due, while also fostering a spirit of generosity. As counselors representing Christ, we are all aiming for the same thing—to love people well and draw them to the gospel. Every creative endeavor should in some way be built off what God has already given us. He is the author of all that is good and true, all that is winsome and creative and beautiful.

Time and effort are essential to cultivating creativity. Great ideas and brilliant moments are actually the result of time-consuming work and flow from the joining of ideas, wisdom, experiences, trial and error, etc. We learn and grow by practice and adaptation. Feel free to take the ideas in this book and build on them, develop them, or adapt them, being faithful to use Scripture well and winsomely in the lives of young people. In addition, try your hand at creating new activities. There is so much treasure to glean from God's Word; there are endless truths to share and to impress upon the lives of children and teens.

Working with young people may appear to be an innately God-given gift, but it is really a fostered expertise and aptitude that grows when we commit ourselves to knowing and loving this community well. Let's lean into the truth, wisdom, and encouragement of God's Word as our foundation as we seek to best steward the ministry he has given us. It is a privilege to serve on the front lines of ministry as a counselor, and to seek to winsomely connect a struggling young person to the heartbeat of Christ.

It takes prayer and deliberate thoughtfulness to intentionally draw out and speak into the lives of people. With some populations, it feels easier, more akin to our style and manner of engagement. However, brotherly love always seeks to move toward and understand those who are different than us.

Regardless of the population you work with, be willing to enter into their world. Seek to know and understand them well. It is my prayer that all of us would desire to live out Ephesians 5:1–2 in the way we engage with others: "Therefore be imitators of God, as beloved children. And walk in love, as Christ loved us and gave himself up for us, a fragrant offering and sacrifice to God."

Appendix A

Sample Developmental Charts

There are many models of development that organizations follow, whether it is among medical professionals, education and learning specialists, or counseling professionals. These sample lists have been created for the purpose of one-on-one counseling ministry with children.

Development is broken down in the five developmental stages: early, middle, late childhood, young teen, and teenager. Such divisions are flexible, and based on the observations of large populations of children. (For this reason, we have broken out early childhood into two separate lists.) Each stage has general milestones that give you a sense for where a child might fall, but there is always a spectrum that allows for various rates of development. It is an ongoing process, to be regularly evaluated.

EARLY CHILDHOOD MILESTONES (AGES 3–4)

Physical

- ✓ Learns to hold utensils and writing tools
- ✓ Draws lines and circles
- ✓ Runs, skips, climbs independently
- ✓ Can pedal
- ✓ Able to start dressing themselves
- ✓ Demonstrates dominant hand
- ✓ Can use toilet on their own
- ✓ Is aware of gender

Emotional

- ✓ Can tell what is real and make-believe
- ✓ Shows more independence and preferences
- ✓ Perceives world from self point of view
- ✓ Likes to imitate parents or caregivers
- ✓ Identifies basic emotions
- ✓ Identity and security established by caregivers
- ✓ Becoming more social and likes making friends

Cognitive

- ✓ Can count to ten or more
- ✓ More literal and concrete in understanding
- ✓ Talks in sentences
- ✓ Unable to see perspectives other than own
- ✓ Begins to understand cause and effect
- ✓ Can formulate own ideas and questions
- ✓ Recites songs, rhymes, and simple stories
- ✓ Shows own preferences, likes, and dislikes
- ✓ Can complete puzzles and memory games
- ✓ Attention span often 5–10 minutes

Social

- ✓ Inner world is expressed through play
- ✓ Enters into role-play
- ✓ Can follow simple games and simple rules
- ✓ Learns to take turns
- ✓ Begins to learn cooperation and sharing
- ✓ Bonds with a friend
- ✓ Notices the physical world around them
- ✓ Tests authority, demonstrates own will

Spiritual

- ✓ Learns right and wrong by example
- ✓ Conscience is undeveloped, shaped by what is modeled
- ✓ Obedience toward God is patterned in obedience to parents
- ✓ Understands simple truths in concrete ways
- ✓ Literal understanding of God, heaven, sin, obedience, kindness, and sharing
- ✓ Good and bad behavior often understood through attached consequences

Helpful Resources:

Puppet sand miniatures

Role-play scenarios and tools

Art materials: blank paper, markers, crayons, glue, etc.

Dollhouse for identifying family roles, rules, patterns

Musical instruments for self-expression

Books, pictures, and the use of storytelling to deliver messages and understanding

EARLY CHILDHOOD MILESTONES (AGES 5–6)

Physical

- ✓ Speaks clearly
- ✓ Shares simple stories
- ✓ Greater use of imagination
- ✓ Able to learn to ride a bike
- ✓ Can fully dress themselves
- ✓ Able to tie shoes
- ✓ Begins to learn letters and shapes

Emotional

- ✓ Can begin to demonstrate empathy
- ✓ Shows more independence and preferences
- ✓ Shows wide range of emotions
- ✓ Becoming more social and likes making friends
- ✓ Learning impulse control
- ✓ Anxiety and emotions demonstrate in play and fantasy
- ✓ Reality and fantasy can blend together
- ✓ Starts to verbalize feelings of doubt, guilt, shame, embarrassment

Cognitive

- ✓ Greater awareness of outside world
- ✓ Greater awareness of cause and effect outside of themselves
- ✓ Can tell what is real and make-believe
- ✓ Can begin to do simple problem solving
- ✓ Follows multiple steps/directions
- ✓ Growing sense of time
- ✓ Remember words and events associated with touching, smelling, and hearing, as well as with emotions (both pleasant and fearful)
- ✓ Attention span averages 10–15 minutes

Social

- ✓ Learning cooperation in groups
- ✓ May be part of a group but not interact much because they see themselves first
- ✓ Enjoys structured play and games
- ✓ Can follow rules and likes to make others follow them
- ✓ Wants everything to be fair—this is where temper tantrums may come in
- ✓ Shows more independence in relationship-building
- ✓ Relationships built on common likes
- ✓ Wants to be liked and accepted
- ✓ Can begin to exhibit competition

Spiritual

- ✓ Knows that the Bible is an important book about God's people and Jesus
- ✓ Enjoys stories about Jesus and likes to hear stories over and over again
- ✓ Develops a sense of church community and attendance
- ✓ Benefits from accepting adults who are willing to hear their many questions

✓ Asks many questions: Where is God? Does he eat? Who made God? Why is God invisible?

✓ Learns easy, simple prayers

✓ Can be encouraged to give their own offering to God and the church

✓ Relies on authority for their moral compass

✓ Conscience regarding sin and behavior is developing

✓ Experiencing and enjoying God's world

Helpful Resources:

Art Materials: colored pencils, crayons, markers, glue, simple crafts

Object lessons to help deliver a message or truth

Puppets, miniatures, or dollhouses/sand trays—role-playing and personal application

Simple games for asking questions, role-playing, or real-life scenarios to work through

Books and stories that help delve into and reaffirm a message/truth

Musical instruments for telling or creating their own stories or songs

Other concrete ways to convey the message/truth you want to affirm

MIDDLE CHILDHOOD MILESTONES (AGES 7–9)

Physical

- ✓ Have adult teeth and growing appetite

- ✓ Active and enjoys sports/activities

- ✓ Improved coordination and strength

- ✓ Able to draw more complex pictures with objects, people, and animals

- ✓ Handwriting and hand-eye coordination improves

- ✓ Speech is clear and vocabulary increases greatly

- ✓ With growing numbers of kids, puberty may develop (around age 9)

Emotional

- ✓ Likes affection and affirmation from adults

- ✓ Peer influence is growing and shaping likes/dislikes

- ✓ Can articulate many emotions and feelings

- ✓ Growing autonomy from parents in many skills and abilities

- ✓ Demonstrates greater ability to control impulses and think before acting

- ✓ May be more argumentative and willful

Cognitive

- ✓ Can begin to understand more abstract ideas

- ✓ Can think more systematically; able to generalize what is learned

- ✓ Considers more questions and becomes more curious about life

- ✓ Amply verbal

- ✓ Enjoys humor and laughter

- ✓ Increases ability to recall events and remember sequence

- ✓ Able to spell out words and read books

- ✓ Attention span varies but averages 15 minutes

Social

- ✓ Often will prefer same-sex peer group

- ✓ Enjoys social interactions and group activities

- ✓ Leadership and status in social groups begin to emerge

- ✓ Begins to look for sense of belonging in the peer group

- ✓ Wants peer approval

- ✓ Can enjoy time alone

- ✓ Group identity affirmed by likes: sports, music, art

- ✓ Begins to form hobbies and interests

Spiritual

- ✓ Will be curious, asking never-ending questions while exploring God's world

- ✓ Practices love and trust as a result of parents or other significant adults; begins to understand God's love

- ✓ Able to see battle to see things "my way" or "God's way"

- ✓ Can be rule-oriented (i.e., "follow the rules and you are good"—instead of "Jesus makes us good")

✓ Learns that parents obey God, and that they too must obey God

✓ Develops empathy and love for others and toward new people

✓ Imitates and repeats what a parent does

✓ Consistency becomes one of the most important qualities for moral and spiritual development

✓ Strong sense of fairness; proneness to being pharisaical

✓ Personal relationship to God develops, exhibited by asking God for help, change, do what's right

✓ Recognizes others' poor behavior and sin

Helpful Resources:

Working with concrete objects, instead of just images

Stories and books which capture the interest of the child and help develop a sense of wonder and awe

Art materials, to continue to draw out and engage with ideas

Creating spaces or worlds (fantasy or real) to engage with hard feelings, events, or ideas

Storytelling through song, music, books, role-play

Concrete projects/ideas/homework for parents, to practice new truths or things they are learning in the home or school environment

Creative tools like balls or Jenga that have questions and role-playing scenarios—fosters conversation and processing of hard things while doing something enjoyable

LATE CHILDHOOD MILESTONES (AGES 10–12)

Physical

- ✓ Energetic and active
- ✓ Height and weight increase progressively
- ✓ Body begins to go through changes
- ✓ Developing body proportions similar to those of an adult
- ✓ May begin puberty—evident sexual development, voice changes, and increased body odor are common
- ✓ Skin becomes oiler and may develop pimples
- ✓ Hair grows in various areas of the body

Emotional

- ✓ Fluctuates between confidence and insecurity
- ✓ Begins to define self by the way others see them
- ✓ Ability to see differing views
- ✓ Greater fluctuating emotions and moodiness
- ✓ Distinguishes between will, actions, and motives
- ✓ Is more aware of strengths and weaknesses

Cognitive

- ✓ Increased ability to learn and apply skills
- ✓ Establishes abstract thinking skills, but reverts to concrete thought under stress
- ✓ Not yet able to make all intellectual leaps, like inferring a hypothetical motive or reason
- ✓ Learns to extend thinking beyond personal experiences and knowledge
- ✓ View of the world extends beyond a black-white/right-wrong perspective
- ✓ Interpretative ability develops
- ✓ Able to answer who, what, where, and when questions, but still may have problems with why questions
- ✓ Attention span varies widely; averages 20 minutes at a time

Social

- ✓ Increased ability to interact with peers
- ✓ Often struggles with relating to peers, either by being controlled or trying to control peers
- ✓ Looks for acceptance through peer group
- ✓ Increased capacity to engage in competition
- ✓ Has a strong group identity; increasingly defines self through peers
- ✓ Sense of accomplishment based upon the achievement of increased strength and self-control
- ✓ Shows more interest in the opposite sex
- ✓ Imagines self as an adult and independent
- ✓ Defines self-concept in part by success in school
- ✓ Able to understand and engage with the emotions and struggles of others
- ✓ Able to learn and apply conflict resolution skills

Spiritual

- ✓ Develops and tests values and beliefs that will guide present and future behaviors
- ✓ Aware of internal conscience and motives influencing choices and behaviors
- ✓ Pursuit of God's help often linked to meeting needs and help with relationships
- ✓ Identifies discrepancies in values of others and compares/contrasts them to own values
- ✓ Can discern between their desires toward sin and desire to follow God

- ✓ Struggles how to think and respond to being sinned against by others
- ✓ Begins questioning rules, while maintaining that rules are important and to be followed
- ✓ Struggles to know how God sees them versus how others see them
- ✓ Needs to be taught how to pray and what to expect when they pray

Helpful Resources:

Journaling and self-reflection activities

Question-asking games

Games that foster godly conflict resolution and working through difficult situations

Role-playing exercises

Bible studies and resources that foster personal relationship with the Lord

Worksheets and group activities that facilitate mature discussions of hard issues

Storytelling; testimonies; real, personal examples of change, faith, and growth

Strategic games that work on problem solving

Art materials and resources

YOUNG TEEN MILESTONES (AGES 13–14)

Physical

- ✓ Hormones change as puberty begins
- ✓ More concerned about physical changes and appearance
- ✓ Eating increases and changes, and at times eating problems develop
- ✓ Physical activity important for health and general mood
- ✓ Requires more sleep, but often resists it
- ✓ Development of sexual organs and voice change

Emotional

- ✓ Experiences more moodiness
- ✓ Demonstrates more concern about appearance, body image, looks
- ✓ Feels more stress and pressure to perform in school
- ✓ Sadness, depression, anxiety related to school performance, peer acceptance, or parental expectations
- ✓ Able to express feelings and talk through them

Cognitive

- ✓ Have more ability for complex thought
- ✓ Able to be abstract
- ✓ Holds own opinions and begins to turn to peers to inform them
- ✓ Needs help considering long-term consequences for choices/decisions, rather than short-term benefits

Social

- ✓ Significantly driven by the value of their peer group
- ✓ Friendships formed around feelings of who accepts them and where they fit in
- ✓ Desires autonomy from parents and greater dependence on peer group
- ✓ Proactive relationship-building with adults is not valued, but much needed
- ✓ Forms connections and bonds over social media

Spiritual

- ✓ Begins to realize choices are complex and that they can choose to sin
- ✓ Rules may or may not be important—temptation to feel they can judge morality
- ✓ May understand the letter of the law more than the spirit of the law
- ✓ Personal relationship with the Lord must lead to decisions/choices
- ✓ Develops stronger individual values and morals
- ✓ Will question more ideas
- ✓ May express discomfort praying out loud, and need help learning to pray and knowing what to expect when they pray
- ✓ Learning to take responsibility for own actions, decisions, and consequences

Helpful Resources:

Question-asking exercises and activities

Resources that help develop good decision-making and godly values

Art activities and resources for self-expression and self-awareness

Activity or exercises that encourage self-expression of feelings, thoughts, and values

Genuine interest in hearing their opinions, likes, dislikes

Forming trust/mutual respect by engaging with or entering their world—social media, art, athletics, hobbies, other interests

TEENAGE MILESTONES (AGES 15–18)

Physical

- ✓ Physical abilities at their peak
- ✓ Completion of puberty from childhood
- ✓ Females tend to reach adult height, while males continue to grow
- ✓ Increased muscle strength, reaction time, cardio functioning, and sensory abilities
- ✓ Changes of skin, vision, and reproductive ability
- ✓ Begins expressing sexuality in various ways
- ✓ Requires more sleep and proper nutrition
- ✓ Greater physical independence: learns to drive, gets a job, spends time with friends

Emotional

- ✓ Can articulate their own feeling and analyze why they feel a certain way
- ✓ Wrestles with understanding what drives their emotions/motives
- ✓ Develops their own personality and opinions
- ✓ Attributes values on appearance, talents, and personality
- ✓ Capable of intense emotions and mood changes

Cognitive

- ✓ Decision-making is still developing
- ✓ Learning choices have risks and consequences
- ✓ Builds self-sufficiency skills
- ✓ Sometimes struggles to think through risks and consequences of actions
- ✓ Brain still developing and maturing
- ✓ Forms well-defined work habits
- ✓ Considers and makes plans for the future: school, college, job

Social

- ✓ Demonstrates loyalty to peer group
- ✓ Desires increased independence from parents/family
- ✓ Influenced by choices, values, and habits of peer group
- ✓ More concerns about body image and clothes
- ✓ Greater capacity for caring for others
- ✓ Challenges parental authority, with desire to be more autonomous
- ✓ Has the capacity to form deep, mutual, healthy relationships
- ✓ Influenced by cultural values and messages
- ✓ Greater ability to sense right and wrong
- ✓ May feel more sadness and emotion—can lead to poor grades, use of addictive substances, and other problems

Spiritual

✓ Wants ways to make faith relevant to life

✓ Confused by cultural norms and values versus biblical values

✓ Corporate worship and church attendance critical to shaping values and forming a personal relationship with Christ

✓ May express discomfort praying out loud, and needs help learning to pray and knowing what to expect when they pray

✓ Godly, healthy adult relationships vital to spiritual development

✓ Needs modeling of how to deal with peer pressure and issues of addiction, sexuality, and suicide

✓ Benefits from adult-led discussions and opportunities to ask questions

Helpful Resources:

Question-asking exercises and activities

Resources that help develop good decision-making and mature choices

Resources that instill godly values and mature relationships

Stories, testimonies, and personal examples of people who have overcome hard issues teens face, providing examples that guide toward godliness and faith

Art activities and resources for self-expression and self-awareness

Activity or exercises that encourage self-expression of feelings, thoughts, and values

Genuine interest in hearing their opinions, likes, dislikes

Forming trust/mutual respect by engaging with or entering their world—social media, art, athletics, hobbies, other interests

Creating places of supportive community

Fostering safe discussion and opportunity for questions on topics of peer friendships, drugs and alcohol, sex, depression, and suicide

Notes

1.Michael R. Emlet, *Cross Talk: Where Life & Scripture Meet* (Greensboro, NC: New Growth Press, 2009).

2. Colin Fernandez, "Adulthood Begins at 30: Scientists Say That Our Brains Are Not Fully Grown-up When We Are in Our Twenties," *The Daily Mail*, March 18, 2019, https://www.dailymail.co.uk/sciencetech/article-6824499/Adulthood-begins-30-Scientists-say-brains-not-fully-grown-twenties.html.

3. Julie Lowe, *Child Proof: Parenting by Faith, Not Formula* (Greensboro, NC: New Growth Press, 2018).

4. Charles Spurgeon, "Bringing Sinners to the Savior," Sermon No. 2731, *The Complete Works of C. H. Spurgeon* (Harrington, DE: Delmarva Publications, 2013).

5. William Gibson, *The Miracle Worker*, dir. Arthur Penn (Los Angeles: Playfilm Productions, 1962), motion picture.

6. Association for Play Therapy, "Why Play Therapy?" https://www.a4pt.org/page/CopyofWhyPlayThera.

7. Richard Louv, *Last Child in the Woods: Saving Our Children from Nature-Deficit Disorder* (New York: Workman Publishing, 2005).

8. Dr. Seuss, *My Many Colored Days* (New York: Random House, 1996).

9. Max Lucado, *You Are Special* (Wheaton, IL: Crossway, 1997).

BUILDING BRIDGES RESOURCES

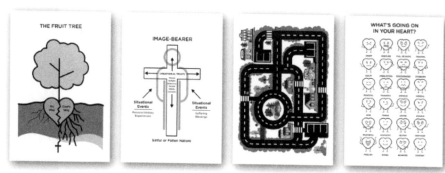

To access printable PDFs of the activity pages from this book, please go to the Building Bridges product page on the New Growth Press website. In the description, there will be a link to access the files. Click on the link and enter the password BuildBridge20.

DATE DUE

Demco, Inc. 38-293